SHOULD I TAKE THE PILL?

Providing Biblical Counsel on Birth Control and Contraceptives

By Sean and Jennifer Perron

Copyright 2022 © Association of Certified Biblical Counselors

All rights reserved.

ISBN: 9798986220529

Taken from *Letters to a Romantic: On Engagement* by Sean Perron and Spencer Harmon.
ISBN: 9781629953076
Used with permission from P&R Publishing Co., P.O. Box 817, Phillipsburg, NJ, 08865.
www.prpbooks.com

Association of Certified Biblical Counselors

As we face the issues of sin and suffering in a broken world, we all need wisdom from God. Thankfully, the Lord has given us all that we need for life and godliness through His sufficient Word (2 Peter 1:3; 2 Timothy 3:16).

ACBC's Truth in Love resources are designed to bring the rich truth of God's character and promises to bear on the problems people face in everyday life. As you walk with others, seeking to minister the very words of God to them, we pray this booklet will be a resource that points you back to His truth and equips you to admonish the idle, encourage the fainthearted, and help the weak (1 Thessalonians 5:14).

Authors
Sean and Jennifer Perron are both ACBC certified counselors, have been married 10 years, and have two children. Sean serves as the Associate Pastor at First Baptist Church in Jacksonville, Florida, holds a specialization in marriage counseling, and is the co-author of the *Letters to a Romantic* series on marriage and dating. Jennifer has a degree in Elementary Education.

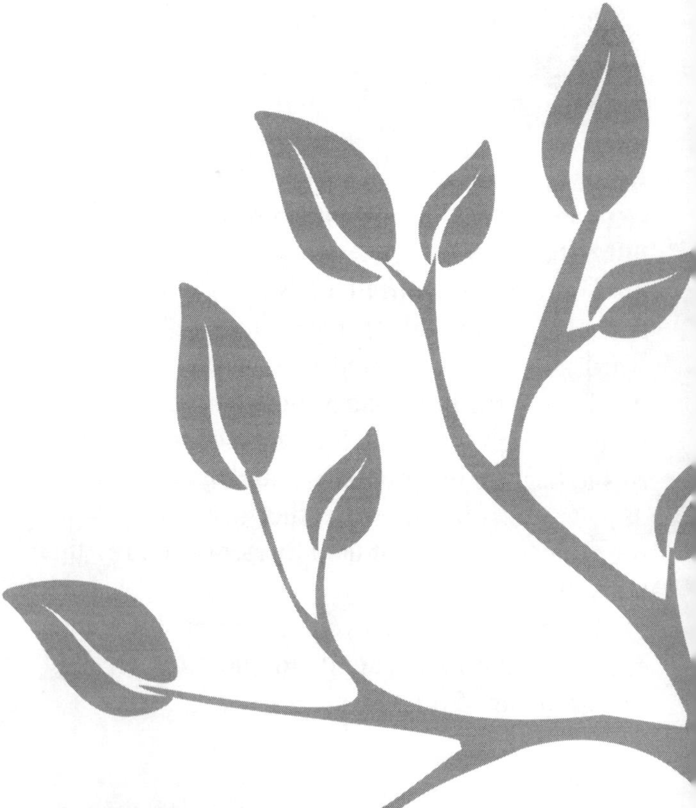

After we got engaged, we encountered all kinds of new life decisions for the first time. We were picking a wedding location, selecting bridal party members, discussing housing options, and we were even talking about how many kids we wanted to have in the future. Yet one of the most critical life decisions we would make was whether Jenny would take the Pill.[1]

I (Jenny) had been on the Pill since high school. For me, taking the Pill was straightforward and uncomplicated. I went to my doctor, and he told me that I had a medical condition that required me to take the Pill consistently in order to have a regular cycle. I did not question his diagnosis nor have any ethical problem with his prescription. It was not until the time for marriage that a re-evaluation of the Pill was necessary in my mind.

By the time Sean and I were engaged, we both discovered that taking the Pill was problematic. We had heard about medical research that called into question whether the Pill was truly a contraceptive because it could be abortive. I had been taking the Pill in order to have regular cycles, but now that marriage was approaching, the question

---

[1] Soon after the birth control pill was introduced to the U.S. market in the 1960s, it became known as simply "the Pill." In this booklet, we use "the Pill" to refer to oral contraceptives and the term birth control more broadly to include various types of contraceptive methods.

of using the Pill as a contraceptive was crucial. We took the possibility that the Pill could cause abortions very seriously. My medical diagnosis added another layer of complexity for us. The Pill had been the solution for my medical problem and to consider stopping it might put me in danger. We knew that Christians disagreed on the subject, and it would require a fresh look at how the Pill works medically and whether it is in keeping with biblical commands.

Over a decade later, we now frequently counsel couples about this very common and relevant issue. Couples preparing for marriage often need to work through hard questions about birth control. It is common that couples who have been married for many years may not have even considered some of these crucial questions.

Biblical counselors must be able to provide biblical answers to the following questions: Is birth control acceptable at all? What makes the Pill unique? What does the Pill do? What factors should women consider before taking the Pill? What about women who have taken the Pill for a long time? What about married women who have medical conditions that require the Pill? These questions, among many others, led us to address the ultimate question for this booklet. How does the Bible instruct us to counsel couples regarding the Pill?

This short booklet is written to provide biblical insights to help Christian couples make wise decisions about birth control in general and the Pill in particular. As Christians, we are called to do everything to the glory of God and it is our prayer that this material serves you and brings God glory as you seek to apply Scripture to this sensitive and significant topic (1 Corinthians 10:31). Once a decision is made about whether to use birth control, another decision must be made about which birth control method. Counselors must carefully explain how some birth control methods are acceptable to God and others are forbidden.

Is Birth Control Acceptable At All?
The Bible is clear that children are a gift from the Lord. "Behold, children are a heritage from the Lord, the fruit of the womb a reward. Like arrows in the hand of a warrior are the children of one's youth. Blessed is the man who fills his quiver with them!" (Psalm 127:3-5). In the book of Genesis, God tells His people on two separate occasions to "be fruitful and multiply" (Genesis 1:28; 9:1). This mentality is drastically different from the average Western mindset. Scripture does not see children as a burden. Rather, the Bible views children as a blessing and delight.

While it is true that sex is designed to produce children, procreation is not the only reason God created sex. Paul talks about sex within marriage, and in 1 Corinthians 7:5 he writes, "Do not deprive one another, except perhaps by agreement for a limited time, that you may devote yourselves to prayer; but then come together again, so that Satan may not tempt you because of your lack of self-control." The biblical ethicists John and Paul Feinburg correctly note that God has intended sex as a gift of procreation, companionship, unity, pleasure, and a means of curbing fornication and adultery.[2] We are not convinced the Bible requires married couples to have the intentionality or willingness to getting pregnant each time they have sex. The Scriptures encourage believers to have sex frequently in marriage and not just when a wife is fertile.

The issue of whether Christians can ethically use birth control can be complicated because of sinful heart desires. Believers must be very careful not to be selfish in their sexual motives. Often career pursuits, high standards of living, idolatrous financial concerns, and laziness are the reasons people use birth control. It is selfish for a couple to use birth control because they do not want the hassle of children. This, however, does

---

[2] John Feinberg and Paul Feinberg, *Ethics for a Brave New World* (Wheaton, IL: Crossway, 1993), 175-176. The Second Edition of *Ethics for A Brave New World* was published in 2010.

not mean all birth control is intrinsically sinful. There is a distinction between heart motives and the ethical and biblical permissibility of a particular method of birth control. Biblical wisdom is required when couples are deciding how many children they should seek to conceive. There are acceptable reasons for using biblical wisdom for discerning when to have children.

The issue of whether or not to remain single or get married is parallel to the issue of how many children a couple should seek to conceive. Both issues require biblical principles and wisdom in order to make a God glorifying decision. For example, the Bible clearly states that marriage is a good gift from the Lord. "He who finds a wife finds a good thing and obtains favor from the Lord" (Proverbs 18:22). "Then the Lord God said, "It is not good that the man should be alone; I will make him a helper fit for him" (Genesis 2:18). God has declared marriage good! Why would anyone stop this blessing from coming? Therefore, isn't it immoral for someone to choose to remain single? Not necessarily. It all depends on the purpose for remaining single.

The apostle Paul writes "So then he who marries his betrothed does well, and he who refrains from marriage will do even better" (1 Corinthians 7:38). Paul argues very effectively that if a believer decides to remain single for the cause of Christ, then it is actually better to avoid the blessing of marriage. We believe this argument and analogy is appropriate for the discussion of birth control.[3]

It is not hard to imagine certain circumstances and seasons of life that would possibly warrant the regulation of when and how many children should be born. If a couple is overseas in a hostile "closed" country on the mission's field, it might be better for the advancement of the gospel if they had less children. If a couple is very tight on finances and one of the spouses has a couple more years in school, it might be appropriate to exercise wisdom in using certain ethically permissible forms of birth control. First Timothy 5:8 says, "But if anyone does not provide for his relatives, and especially for members of his household, he has denied the faith and is worse than an unbeliever."

Some Christians believe that God alone should be the one to decide when a wife should become pregnant. They argue that birth control is sinful because it expresses a lack of faith in God's sovereignty. We want to be clear that God is completely sovereign over conception and the womb (Ruth 4:13). Nothing happens on earth

---

[3] I first heard this argumentation and idea from an interview with John Piper on Desiring God. This section has been shaped by Piper's writing and thinking. John Piper, "Is it Wrong to Use Birth Control?" March 5, 2008, http://www.desiringgod.org/interviews/is-it-wrong-to-use-birth-control.

without God's appointment and permission. However, this does not mean that the use of biblically legitimate or acceptable means of birth control is necessarily sinful or an outright rejection of God's sovereignty.

In conjunction with God's absolute sovereignty, God holds man responsible. This is a clear teaching of Scripture that should not be ignored (Ecclesiastes 12:13; Romans 3:19; 9:19-20). It is a fallacy to think that planning on how many children you have will hinder God's sovereignty. God will not allow the use of birth control to thwart His eternal plans. God has chosen to give us the mind of Christ to use wisdom and discernment in the cause of advancing His kingdom. This is not contrary to His sovereignty.

While it is true that the Bible says children are a blessing, this does not mean it is ethically right to have as many babies as the wife is physically capable of bearing. John Piper has helpfully noted, "We should make our decisions on Kingdom purposes. If—for Kingdom reasons, gospel reasons, advancement reasons, and radical service reasons—having another child would be unwise then I think we have the right and the freedom to regulate that."[4] These biblically informed reasons lead us to conclude that the Bible does not forbid non-abortifacient

---

[4] John Piper, "Is it Wrong to Use Birth Control?"

forms of birth control as long as it is used selflessly and for the glory of God.

When counseling couples about their decision to prevent pregnancy, the first category to work through is the heart motivations behind using birth control. Is each spouse in agreement about the motivation behind using it? Are the intentions of the couple biblically formed or conformed to the world? Are the desires of the heart self-centered or God-centered?

Once a decision is made about whether to use birth control, another decision must be made about which birth control method. Counselors must carefully explain how some birth control methods are acceptable to God and others are forbidden. This category of conversations is about safe versus dangerous methods. Are the methods honoring life or harming life?

God alone is the giver and taker of human life (1 Samuel 2:6). Scripture clearly teaches that life begins before birth. The Bible teaches that life begins at the moment of conception. Conception is the moment when the sperm and the egg meet. In the book of Psalms, David recognized that he was a human being at the moment of conception. Biblical texts include verses like Psalm 51:5, Psalm 139, Genesis 25:22, and Luke 1:41. In God's eyes, a blastocyst is just as human as a seventy-year-old man. Therefore, when a person considers birth control, it is imperative that they do not use methods that destroy life after the woman's egg has been fertilized.[5]

The accurate definition of contraception is "against conception." Contraceptives prevent the sperm and egg from ever uniting. There are several methods that prevent conception such as the condom, diaphragm, cervical cap, and various creams and jellies. Some have argued that it is immoral to use "artificial" methods of contraception and that only "natural" methods should be used. Natural methods can include the calendar method, temperature method, or withdrawal method (coitus interruptus). The main objections to using artificial barrier methods are that they have the potential to be romantically inconvenient and may place an unnecessary barrier between couples during their most intimate moment. It may be ideal to use natural methods, but there is nothing direct in Scripture, or even in scriptural principle, to say that artificial contraceptives are immoral. As long as they are used selflessly, artificial methods do not distort the biblical picture of Christ and his bride.[6]

---

[5] See also Sarah Terzo, "40 Quotes from Medical Experts and Textbooks that Prove Human Life Begins at Fertilization," June 3, 2016, https://www.liveaction.org/news/40-quotes-from-medical-experts-that-prove-human-life-begins-at-conception/?gclid=CjwKCAiA9ty-QBhAIEiwA6tdCrK6SuOgTNF8haxETdZL1piKKvtwe-GEyN0IJgB5dTJqB616TTmi4k4hoCLa0QAvD_BwE.

[6] An argument can be made that there is more of an ethical

The current definition of contraception can be deceiving. Again, the Feinburgs are helpful in their summary of how artificial contraception works. They write, "Artificial means of contraception generally work in one of three ways. Either they prevent fertilization of the ovum by the sperm altogether, or they prevent a fertilized egg from attaching to the wall of the uterus, or they destroy the embryo after implantation."[7] When either the egg is prevented from implanting or the embryo is destroyed as a result, then these specific contraception methods are considered abortifacients. It is abortion when a fertilized egg is unable to attach itself to the uterine wall due to an artificial birth control method. Without the ability of implantation, this new life will be flushed out with the next menstrual cycle.

Much confusion arises because many doctors include some abortifacients within the broader category of contraceptives. The pro-life

---

concern with the natural monthly abstinence method of birth control than there is against artificial methods. The Bible takes breaking the sexual routine in marriage seriously. The only stated reason Paul allows a short period of sexual abstinence in marriage is for the purpose of prayer (1 Corinthians 7:5). There are more exceptions to this rule (such as deployment and sickness) and it is possible that avoiding pregnancy could be included in this. However, it cannot be biblically argued that couples must avoid sex during a woman's fertile window in order to favor of natural birth control over artificial birth controls.

[7] *Ethics for a Brave New World*, 170.

position argues that methods such as "the morning after pill" and the "mini pill" are abortive in function because they do not permit the blastoyst to implant on the uterine wall. This also includes Intrauterine Devices (IUD's) which thin the lining of the uterine wall to prevent implantation.[8] If Christians are to use artificial birth control, they must be sure that their method is strictly contraceptive and not abortive. God is explicit that murder is not morally permissible (Exodus 20:13; Matthew 5:21-26). This leads to the crucial question: Is the Pill a contraceptive method of birth control or an abortive method?

---

[8] Intrauterine Devices (IUDs) are similar to the Pill in that they are not exclusively a contraceptive. They have an abortive function in addition to contraceptive functions. Just like the Pill, information about IUDs in the medical community can be deceptive because they are often labeled a contraceptive. However, asking a few clarifying questions and doing a little more research quickly shows that they have a significant abortive function. See The Free Dictionary, "IUD", https://medical-dictionary.thefreedictionary.com/IUD. Planned Parenthood is eager to promote the contraceptive elements of IUDs, but fail to mention how it prevents implantation as well. Yet even Planned Parenthood describes IUDs as an "emergency contractive" that effectively prevents pregnancy after sex. Planned Parenthood still calls it a contraceptive, but they do not cover up the reality that it kills a fertilized egg after sex. Planned Parenthood, "IUD," https://www.plannedparenthood.org/learn/birth-control/iud.

What Makes the Birth Control Pill Unique?

It should be noted that there are several risks involved for the consumer of the Pill. When the Pill first emerged, the main concerns were with blood-clotting, strokes, and cancer.[9] In the 2000's, fears arose about the potential side effects of breast, ovary, and endometrial cancer. Some women do not take the Pill because of painful headaches, mood swings, lack of sex drive, or heart disease.[10] Since 2020, more health concerns have been raised and there is a growing movement among secular medical professionals to find alternatives for the Pill.[11]

While these risks are significant, they are secondary to the main ethical concern at stake, whether the Pill is a potential abortifacient. Most people are told that the Pill is simply a contraceptive because it prevents ovulation and does not allow the eggs to be fertilized. However, because this statement is not completely factual, it is also

---

[9] Bernard Asbell, *The Pill: A Biography of the Drug that Changed the World* (New York, NY: Random House, 1995), 304-305.

[10] Sandra Glahn and Wiliam Cutrer, *The Contraception Guidebook: Options, Risks, and Answers for Christian Couples* (Grand Rapids, MI: Zondervan, 2005), 98.

[11] Sarah E. Hill, *This is Your Brain on Birth Control: The Surprising Science of Women, Hormones, and the Law of Unintended Consequences* (New York, NY: Avery, 2019); Jolene Brighten, *Beyond the Pill: A 30-Day Program to Balance Your Hormones, Reclaim Your Body, and Reverse the Dangerous Side Effects of the Birth Control Pill* (New York, NY: HarperOne, 2019).

misleading. It is true that the Pill's main purpose is contraceptive, but this is not the only purpose of the Pill.

The Pill is a very effective means of pregnancy prevention. It is rather rare that someone becomes pregnant while on the Pill. Statistics range from 1%-4.7% of women who become pregnant even though they consistently and accurately used the Pill. While this seems like a successful method to the Pill's manufacturers, this statistic is a startling and horrifying fact.

What Does the Pill Do?

Many people, including sincere pro-life Christians, are unaware that the Pill uses three types of birth control mechanisms. The Physicians Desk Reference explains the different functions of the Pill:

> Combination oral contraceptives act by suppression of gonadotropins. Although the primary mechanism of this action is inhibition of ovulation, other alterations include changes in the cervical mucus, which increase the difficulty of sperm entry into the uterus, and changes in the endometrium, which reduce the likelihood of implantation.[12]

---

[12] The *Physicians Desk Reference* is quoted in Randy Alcorn's helpful book *Does the Birth Control Pill Cause Abortions?* For those who want a detailed study on this topic, I strongly recommend this book. It is available for

Medical language notwithstanding, the Pill does three things:

1) Prevents ovulation and thereby prevents conception.

2) Increases mucus which does not permit the sperm and egg to unite .

3) Thins the lining of the uterus, which can prevent a fertilized egg from implanting and thereby being unable to continue to live.

The first two mechanisms of the Pill are contraceptive. If this were all that the Pill accomplished, then there would be no moral controversy. However, the third mechanism of the Pill is abortive in its function. The third function of the Pill is to weaken the uterine wall and reduce the chances of an already fertilized egg (human life) from implanting on the wall. If the fertilized egg cannot implant, it will die.

How Is the Pill Dangerous?

We would affirm the Pill if it was only a contraceptive. A contraceptive prevents the sperm and the egg from uniting. All barrier methods such as

---

free from Eternal Perspective Ministries: https://www.epm.org/static/uploads/downloads/bcpill.pdf; See also William F. Colliton, Jr. M.D, "The Birth Control Pill: Abortifacient and Contraceptive," http://uffl.org/vol10/colliton10.pdf.

condoms and diaphragms are true contraceptives. An abortifacient kills the fertilized egg after it is already conceived. This is literally a life and death difference. Considering this evidence, the question must be asked, "How often do the first two mechanisms fail and the third succeed?"

To answer this question, it is helpful to know that every year 420,000 babies are born despite their mothers taking the Pill. For someone to become pregnant while on the Pill, it means that all three mechanisms of birth prevention have failed. The troubling reality is that we do not know how many times the first two contraceptive mechanisms failed, and the third abortive mechanism worked. We simply do not know how many times the third mechanism takes the life of an unborn child.

Randy Alcorn asks the question, "How many children failed to implant in that inhospitable environment who would have implanted in a nurturing environment unhindered by the Pill?"[13] He then postulates that if the number of deaths was twice the number of babies born then there would be 840,000 deaths a year because of the Pill.

But what if there were only 100,000 deaths a year due to the third mechanism of the Pill? Or what if there were only 10 deaths a year? Would this be morally justifiable? A husband and wife

---

[13] Alcorn Randy, *Does the Birth Control Pill Cause Abortions?*

cannot play Russian roulette with a child's life every time they have sex.

The danger seems distant because the danger is unseen to couples. The danger can feel more like an inconvenience than a real threat. However, the danger is real and present to children in the womb. The Pill places children in an objectively dangerous scenario that thoughtful Christians would not permit if their children were outside the womb. Given the moral complications with the Pill, it should not be used by Christian couples for birth control.

Further Considerations
The abortive potential of the Pill removes it as an ethical birth control option for Christian couples. While this conclusion is straightforward, there are questions, scenarios, and implications that must be further addressed. This last section of the booklet will address a few of the more nuanced and delicate facets of this discussion.

First, for committed Christian women who are single, the morally problematic aspects of the Pill are non-issues. A single Christian woman does not need to worry about the effects of a potentially abortive medication if she is not sexually active. If there are numerous medical conditions that could be helped by the Pill, she should feel free to consult with her physician about its use for those medicinal purposes. She does not need to fear the deadly risk of the Pill for children because she is not placing any children in danger. The main moral dilemma of the Pill is for women who are sexually active.

Second, there are single women who have been on the Pill for years and then get engaged. Those who are engaged to be married (or about to be engaged) should consult with a physician as soon as possible about how to stop taking the Pill if they are currently on it. It is important that engaged women on the Pill begin this transition sooner than they might think. It can take weeks to months for the effects of the Pill to leave a woman's body. A couple should not assume they can stop taking the Pill the day before their wedding night and it will remove the danger of an abortion. It can take time for the Pill's effects to be flushed from a woman's body and her cycle to return to normal. Medical research is always developing, and each woman's body is different.

Some doctors believe it only takes an average of three days for the effects of the Pill to leave a woman's body. Others estimate it can take one to three months. Given the uncertainty of how long it takes to ensure that the uterine wall is not impacted by the Pill, we recommend engaged couples to address this issue as soon as possible before marriage. Married women who are getting off the Pill can use a barrier method during the time when their bodies are adjusting after they stop taking Pill.

Third, what about married women who have medical conditions that are helped the Pill? Some women take the Pill for symptom management and issues related to menstruation regulation such as amenorrhea (absence of menstruation) and dysmenorrhea (frequent menstruation). There are diagnosed medical conditions that are helped by women taking the Pill. These conditions include but are not limited to endometriosis, polycystic ovarian syndrome (PCOS), and primary ovarian insufficiency (POI). In some cases, a medical condition such as endometriosis can have complications that threaten the life of the mother if it is left untreated. The life of a woman is equally important as the life of a baby. We should do everything we can to protect both and uphold life in all circumstances. If a married woman has a medical condition that is so severe that it requires the Pill to keep her from danger, alternative methods of birth control during ovulation should be pursued.

The window of danger for a potential abortion is during the time of a woman's ovulation. It is during that window of time that true contraceptives (such as a barrier method) should be used by the couple even though the wife is taking the Pill. By using a true contraceptive during the window of ovulation, it prevents a pregnancy from possibly being terminated by the Pill.

This requires an additional step of tracking the fertile window of time, but it is an important step. The Pill makes tracking the window of ovulation predictable and this is convenient for predicting the time of ovulation. One important note is that sperm can stay alive for up to five days inside the uterus.[14] This means the window of time for using a barrier method should start earlier than ovulation in order to prevent active sperm from fertilizing an egg while on the Pill.

Protecting the life of the mother is not at odds with protecting the lives of the unborn. All this counsel is meant to pursue life. It does not have to be burdensome. Any extra steps for more complicated scenarios should be done to love God and the neighbors in the womb. A couple can happily enjoy each other while also delight in protecting the unborn.

Finally, the issue of married couples who have been unaware of the danger of the Pill must not be overlooked. Unfortunately, the information contained in this booklet is often breaking news for many couples. Some couples have been sexually active for years without realizing the potential abortions that have taken

---

[14] The Mayo Clinic, "How long do sperm live after ejaculation?", https://www.mayoclinic.org/healthy-lifestyle/getting-pregnant/expert-answers/pregnancy/faq-20058504.

place. This news is heartbreaking and nearly overwhelming for some people. What counsel can be given to married women who have taken the Pill for a long time?

There can be a mixture of emotions in response to this information. Some people want to deny the reality and can't believe this information is true. They question every part of it until they do the research themselves. Others are angry at their Christian parents or church for not teaching them about how to protect life in the womb. Some couples are filled with guilt and don't know how to make things right.

This is an opportunity for counselors to bring light, hope, and relief through the gospel of Jesus. It is the truth that sets us free. We should never be afraid of the truth. Rather, we should run to the truth and embrace God in all His love. Jesus is the way, the truth, and the life (John 14:6). Every couple who encounters this information can find comfort and freedom in the person and work of Christ.

It is also helpful to point out that while we are responsible for our actions, we often don't know what happened in the past when it comes to this issue. We can be honest about what we know and don't know. We know the Pill is potentially abortive when couples are sexually active. We know it does cause some abortions. But we do not know when those abortions occur or how often they occur.

It is possible, that in the kindness and sovereignty of God, a couple might have been sexually active on the Pill for a while and an abortion didn't take place. It is also possible they caused many abortions. We truly don't know. But God knows. God knows and He loves us, cares for us, and forgives us. We can trust Him with this unknown information and rest in His grace.

The Bible teaches that we are responsible for sin. This includes sins whether we intended to disobey or not. Even if we did not know something was sinful, we are still responsible for it. This is why there was a sacrifice required in the Old Testament for sins not intentionally committed (Leviticus 4:1-35; Numbers 15:22-31; Luke 12:47-48). The good news of Jesus is that He forgives us and cleanses us from all sin (1 John 1:9). On the cross He even cried out to God, "Father, forgive them, they know not what they do" (Luke 23:34). Jesus forgives us for every known and unknown sin, and we must trust Him with this. There are countless couples who upon discovering this information, confessed their sin, repented, and found peace. Anyone can receive forgiveness for the past and ask God to help them to act responsibly now with this information (Proverbs 28:13).

How Should Biblical Counselors Engage This Issue?

The best way to address this issue is proactively. The sooner you can get ahead of this problem the better. Counselors should incorporate this information into their church's pre-marital curriculum.[15] It also can be addressed tactfully in pro-life initiatives such as Sanctity of Human Life Sunday. The more church members are made aware of this issue in advance of marriage, the more lives can be saved, and heartache avoided.

Counselors must actively engage couples on this issue sensitively and tenderly. Counselors should approach this issue with care, confidence, and compassion. It is best to seek slow transformation with progress rather than a quick rush to fix the issue.

We must admit that the culture has been winning this war for a long time, and Christians have not adequately addressed this issue. This makes the job of a counselor difficult. It means that patience, love, and care are crucial for helping your counselee understand this issue. Proverbs 16:21–25 should inform our counsel:

---

[15] For a short entry level explanation on birth control for couples to read during engagement, see *Letters to a Romantic: On Engagement* by Sean Perron and Spencer Harmon.

> The wise of heart is called discerning, and sweetness of speech increases persuasiveness. Good sense is a fountain of life to him who has it, but the instruction of fools is folly. The heart of the wise makes his speech judicious and adds persuasiveness to his lips. Gracious words are like a honeycomb, sweetness to the soul and health to the body. There is a way that seems right to a man, but its end is the way to death.

Your authority as a counselor for this issue must rest completely upon the Scripture. Counselors are not the authority on life and death—God is. A counselor must appeal to the Scriptures and explain passages about when life begins and why the Pill threatens life.

Counselors can feel paralyzed by the medical aspect of this issue. But you should remember that science always comes under the authority of Christ. This is an opportunity for you to help counselees to understand the difference between observable science and interpretive "science." Science that is observable, testable, and repeatable will always point people to the truth of God's word and will not contradict it. You can appeal to medical science and research in order to persuade couples of this reality. If you know of medical doctors within your church, be sure to speak with them and use their knowledge. It can be powerfully persuasive if a doctor in your church is willing to speak with your counselees.

When counselees are speaking with their medical professionals, encourage them to ask clarifying questions such as: "When do you believe life begins? Does the Pill thin the lining of the uterine wall? Does the Pill prevent implantation? Are there other ways to treat my medical condition besides the Pill?" It can be helpful to encourage couples to do the research on their own and provide resources to them. Tell them to read the fine print on the birth control prescriptions. The information about the mechanisms of the Pill is readily available if someone is looking for it.

Conclusion
The most important issue when counseling couples on this matter is getting to the heart of their decision making. It is important to understand why a couple wants to use birth control in general and why they specifically want to take the Pill in particular. The motivations in those decisions cannot be neglected. For most couples, information about the science of the Pill is not the real issue.

Is a couple unwilling to transition off the Pill because there is a lack of knowledge, or is there something deeper? Is there a medical issue that needs to be worked through and addressed? Is it a matter of convenience? Is the Pill the easy option? Is sexual pleasure a driving factor? Is there a perceived sense of empowerment or freedom that comes with the Pill? Is there shame and guilt that are looming over the couple?

The ultimate solution for married couples who are making decisions about the Pill is the gospel of Christ. Jesus loves us so much that He lays down His life to save us (John 3:16; John 15:12–14). He covers all our sin, guilt, shame, and mistakes. He covers them and then enables us to follow Him. Because of his grace, we can lay down our lives, our ease, our convenance, and rescue those who are being led to the slaughter (Proverbs 24:11). It is a great privilege to help others love like Jesus loves.

> "This is my commandment, that you love one another as I have loved you. Greater love has no one than this, that someone lay down his life for his friends. You are my friends if you do what I command you." (John 15:12–14)

PART OF THE BIBLICAL SOLUTIONS SERIES

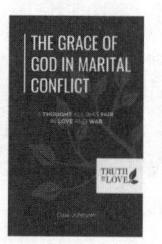

- A Call to Counsel and Care — Samuel Stephens
- The Grace of God in Marital Conflict — Dave Johnson
- The Enneagram and the Biblical Counselor — Shenvi Olimpy
- Child Sexual Abuse: Thinking Biblically About the Unthinkable — Cheryl Bell
- Emotions: Sinful or Sanctified? — Cheryl Bell
- Common Mistakes of Rookie Counselors — Kevin Carson
- Hope for Lasting Change — Samuel Stephens
- The Deception of Psychological Labels: Finding Identity, Responsibility, and Purpose in Jesus Christ
- Suffering: Discerning God's Purposes for Pain — Cheryl Bell
- Fighting Same-Sex Desire: Finding Hope and Freedom in Jesus Christ — Samuel Stephens
- More Coming Soon

GET MORE AT:
biblicalcounseling.com/biblicalsolutions

TRUTH IN LOVE® | ACBC

Biblical Solutions for the Problems People Face

The Association of Certified Biblical Counselors is committed to championing the sufficiency of Scripture for the Church as she engages the problems people face, speaking the truth in love. Christians have the responsibility to bring the truth of God to bear on the problems of everyday life, and to embody that truth in a life of love.

At ACBC, we seek to strengthen the Church to speak the truth in love by providing a quality training and certification process, a global network of like-minded individuals and institutions, and a source of practical and biblical resources for the Church.

In short, we seek to bring *biblical solutions for the problems people face*, upholding that the method God has given to do this is *truth in love*.

Find all our ACBC resources at www.biblicalcounseling.com.

Where the Devil Lost His Poncho

Maggie Pool

The Pentland Press Limited
Edinburgh • Cambridge • Durham • USA

© Maggie Pool 1997

First published in 1997 by
The Pentland Press Ltd.
1 Hutton Close
South Church
Bishop Auckland
Durham

All rights reserved.
Unauthorised duplication
contravenes existing laws.

British Library Cataloguing in Publication Data.
A catalogue record for this book is available
from the British Library.

ISBN 1 85821 460 2

Typeset by CBS, Felixstowe, Suffolk
Printed and bound by Antony Rowe Ltd., Chippenham

To Konrad, constant companion on the
long journey to our lovely back-of-beyond.

ACKNOWLEDGEMENTS

Many thanks are due to my family for their uninhibited suggestions and criticisms of the manuscript and to daughter-in-law Angelica Orduna for her very nice drawings.

My sister Winifred, in far-away Switzerland was particularly helpful and encouraging.

I would also like to thank Sonia Frémery for the basic typescript which reduced the chaos of my first drafts to neatness and order.

In reality, the book is intended as a tribute to Argentina, my second homeland, with personal experiences woven into the colourful, fascinating tapestry that Argentina represents and yet is so little-known to the world at large.

Maggie Pool
June, 1996

CONTENTS

	Illustrations	xi
	Introduction	1
1	Background Data	3
2	Over the Sea to Argentina	20
3	Work and Worship	36
4	Flora and Fauna, among other Things	59
5	Patagonia	99
	References	141

ILLUSTRATIONS

	Map of Argentina	Frontispiece
1	'Long ago and faraway'. Author in Belfast 1924	11
2	My friend Alison	14
3	Ombú	68
4	Oven-bird and nest	69
5	Armadillo	71
6	The family. Buenos Aires 1963	78
7	Author in Tierra del Fuego	100
8	Patagonian steppes	102
9	Volcano Copahue	114
10	Volcano Lanín	129
11	Road through the beech forests	132
12	Lake Traful	137

Introduction

The world is overcrowded, according to the geographic experts, and who am I to contradict?
Nevertheless there are extensive, sparsely populated areas of the earth which are habitable yet practically deserted because people in general seem to want to live among crowds. Long before it occurred to anyone that eventually there would not be enough *lebensraum* to go round, the cities were already crowded. Throughout recorded time, people who preferred the open spaces and country districts to the noisy, stimulating activity of the town, have been popularly regarded as country bumpkins at best and misanthropes at worst.
One of the least densely populated areas of the world today is Argentina, a long land stretching from the Tropic of Capricorn to the Antarctic, with the consequent variety of climate and terrain that this implies. It is true that Buenos Aires and its suburban belt is bursting at the seams with inhabitants. Thirty miles inland, however, the horizon is the limit.
When the Argentine city-dweller wants to refer to some place which in English would be described as the back of beyond, he says: 'there where the devil lost his poncho'. In one of those places, more than a thousand miles south-west of Buenos Aires, on the 42nd parallel South, in one of the many fertile, sheltered Andean valleys, there is a small town called El Bolsón. It is there where I live. Some years ago I joined the growing ranks of city-dwellers who are finding life intolerable in the teeming urban sprawl and are looking to the

smaller towns and the countryside to restore some of the quality that had been sacrificed to modernization and 'progress'. It means changing one set of problems for another, since this side of Paradise there are always problems, but the compensation seems so great that it is well worthwhile.

When I am momentarily out of problems and pottering around the garden feeling grateful for my good fortune, it is tempting to wander back through the years and trace the long journey to this peaceful back of beyond. Far away in the nineteen-twenties in the north of England, the memories begin.

1

Background Data

Some people claim to remember events that occurred when they were one or two years old. Personally I was never able to remember anything concrete before starting school at the age of 5 - no recollection, however hazy, of the journey by boat from Derry to Larne or the train trip to north-east England, or the birth of my sister, or moving into a new house. The first recollection is possibly a dream, or nightmare. In those days no one suspected psychological perturbations or subconscious brain activity as the cause of bad dreams and they were unceremoniously attributed to too much supper, so my parents were not unduly upset over the hair-raising report of this particular nightmare. It culminated in being chased down our garden by an outsize black ostrich which did not reach me because I woke up in time.

Early schooldays have left only a few clear-cut impressions. The mile-long walk in rain, wind and snow remains predominant although even in England there must have been some days of sunshine and warmth. The drawing teacher in the primary school would be surprised and perhaps gratified to know that I can still visualize one of her 'posters' with which she adorned the classroom walls. It represented a vigorous-looking man in cavalier dress draining a tankard and the legend above him was 'onions are good for the blood'. This must have caused me some concern because no one in the family liked onions and we hardly ever ate them.

Schooldays on the whole came back as a constant anxiety, the teachers all seem to have been stern and unlovable, there was despondency at home if I failed to keep within the top half-dozen ('You surely aren't going to let Dorothy beat you!') and I was incapable of writing neatly and free from blots or smudges. The word 'deteriorating' is still a painful reminder that I once wrote what I thought was a good composition only to get an average mark and the heavily emphasized comment in the margin 'Your writing is deteriorating'. I had to look up the word in the dictionary and I can recall the dismay on reading: 'to make or become worse . . .'. Even sports and physical jerks were often a trial because I was a butterfingers with the ball and could never run fast enough.

It would be both inaccurate and unfair to give the impression of an unhappy childhood, but it was a period of intense longings, for the most part unrealized. The dominating passion which obsessed me everywhere and at all times was to own a horse. This was regarded by the family and friends as an unfortunate, inexplicable aberration and too utterly ridiculous to attempt to satisfy. The inevitable reaction after pointing out the obvious financial impossibility involved was: what would I do with a horse? where would I keep it and where could I ride it?

These were valid questions as our house was in the middle of a town but I had a friend who lived on a farm some three miles away and she had told me that if I ever had a horse it could stay there. Beyond the farm, in those days at least, there were fields and country lanes and there was always the mile-long beach with its fine stretch of hard sand.

The financial aspect was a more serious problem but I would gladly have given up music lessons, for instance, or made any kind of sacrifice in clothes and chocolates to have had my horse.

The heaviest blow came when a farmer uncle in Scotland, who was very fond of horses, told he would send me one if my parents would agree. I don't know what they said to him but it must have been on the lines that he was mad, if not raving, and he never brought up the subject again. After that I tried to compromise and suggested just going for riding lessons once a week. Here the financial barricade was raised and I again offered to give up my piano lessons. For some reason, these were inviolable and the ability to play the piano was held to be an essential accomplishment which could give me great satisfaction and joy for the rest of my life, to which riding a horse could never be compared. As things have turned out, I had no piano for over forty years until I inherited one, and although I haven't actually owned a horse either, I had many wonderful hours on horseback both in England during the Second World War and in Argentina where I have lived since 1945.

To set the record straight, however, it has to be remembered that these were the Depression Years, with unemployment and despair the order of the day. My father was never out of work but he was on half-pay for a long time and my mother must have worked miracles with her budget to keep us on an even keel. It is not surprising that the owning of a horse would have seemed an intolerable burden. The fact that eventually my parents were able to buy and run a small car did not signify sudden affluence by any means, and I had to admit that the whole family benefitted from a car whereas a horse would be the selfish pleasure of one member alone.

The longing to ride affected me in many ways. Whenever we went out into the country in the car at weekends, I visualized myself galloping over those wide Northumbrian moors and I would feel almost physical pain if we passed people on horseback, or worse still, met the hunt. My bicycle which I used for going to school and eventually for vacation trips was my make-believe horse and there is no doubt that a child's imagination can be a formidable factor of consolation and a shield against the unrelenting wall of adult incomprehension. I was allowed to buy a magazine on riding and to choose 'horsey' books which simultaneously pleased and tormented me, reading about the lucky people who rode in gymkhanas and had their own ponies and horses.

In my despair I made friends with the milkman's horse and the firewood seller's pony and took them carrots or sugar lumps. As was only to be expected, A.F. Tschiffely became my great hero, an Argentine schoolmaster who rode from Buenos Aires to New York in 1924 with two creole horses, Mancha and Gato. His book *Tschiffely's Ride*, read countless times, has accompanied me everywhere, in fact I still have it. One memorable evening the Great Man Himself gave a lecture in the City Hall of Newcastle-on-Tyne and I was taken to hear him. Not only that, it was somehow arranged for me to go backstage after the lecture and meet him personally. He signed my copy of his book and I probably was prototype of the besotted adolescent in the presence of the idol, the star.

Consolation came to me another way. I had inherited my father's gift for drawing and so I took great pains to learn to draw horses. Progress was very satisfactory but if ever I had to draw a cow or a dog or some other animal, they inevitably looked like horses gone wrong. The drawing which had the most repercussion in family circles was a black ink representation of a four-horse Roman chariot, racing in best Ben-Hur style, which I entered in a children's competition in the *Daily Herald*. That this newspaper, the mouthpiece of the Labour Party, should have found its way into our true-blue conservative household was the result of a momentary cease-fire while my socialist relations from Glasgow were staying with us one summer.

One day the children's page in the newspaper announced a competition in the form of a free-lance drawing and so I drew the thundering quadriga and sent it in, without mentioning the fact to anyone. Great was the sensation when a week later I received a postal order for half a crown as a prize for my effort and with the compliments of the *Daily Herald*. My parents did not know whether to be mortified by the appearance of my name in a socialist newspaper, or gratified that the Labour Party was now half a crown out of pocket to the Conservatives. Recognition of my skill as an artist was thus pushed into the background, overshadowed by politics. I don't even remember what I did with the money which must have been a handsome sum for me in those days.

I collected pictures of horses and pasted them into albums which cluttered up my room. No doubt my parents often wondered when this inexplicable craze would pass, along with other childhood whims. Only on one occasion was I able to try out my theoretical knowledge of riding and I can remember that day in all its details.

My aunt Carrie lived on the other side of the river beyond the industrial zone and on the outskirts of the spreading suburbia. She was friendly with a young lady who owned a riding school nearby and it was arranged that one day I could go for a ride. It was a grey overcast day and I set out, crossed the river in the ferry and took the tram for the long trip out to aunt Carrie's place, in a state of apprehension and excitement which I thought would overwhelm me. I had no riding clothes and at that time blue jeans were unknown in England, so the only alternative was to wear my tartan kilt.

When I arrived at the stables accompanied by my aunt, the owner of the school and one of the instructors looked at me with astonishment. Then they asked me if I had ever ridden before and I said, No, but I had read a lot about it. This remark caused them to laugh heartily and I still hear it and feel the tears not far away. However, they were kind to me. They gave me a quiet brown horse, showed me how to mount correctly and approved of my 'natural hands' - long studied and practised with make-believe reins - and then the three of us set out.

Elation immediately began to gain over my fears and in a few minutes I was trotting properly as if I had been riding for years. This must have been a case of mind over matter, as I was still smarting from the laughter over my naive answer. Just the same I humbly obeyed their instructions because above all I wanted to learn and I could see little hope for another ride in the near or distant future.

The second lesson in fact took place some five years later when I was working away from home, in the autumn of 1940. I had scarcely enough money to live on, let alone pay five shillings an hour for a ride. First I bought a second-hand pair of riding breeches from another girl who found she didn't like the activity. This left me penniless for several weeks and boots were out of the question, but eventually I had five shillings saved up and I went off on my bicycle to the riding school a few miles away. The boots problem was momentarily solved in most unorthodox fashion by using black rubber wellingtons and the old, old dream began to come true.

Another great childhood longing was to live in the country. It was partly related to the desire to own a horse, but on the whole it was due to a particular delight in Nature itself. When we went on vacation we nearly always headed for the hills, the woods and the lakes. The whole family liked the country but always provided good plumbing, as my mother euphemistically would say, was available. It seemed to be a feature of Britain in those days that outside the towns, sanitary facilities were rudimentary, if not distressing, so we remained firmly established among the brick and asphalt of the suburbs, redeemed in our case by the proximity of the sea and sandy beaches.

The real, deep country with stone villages in among the trees and woods, and the lonely, beautiful moors with heather and bracken and springy turf were accessible enough in the car. It is the memory of the unspoiled countryside of Northumberland, the Lake District and Scotland that awakens a melancholy nostalgia for something I could only taste occasionally, even when I lived in Britain.

We became very familiar with the 'brave Borderland' – Northumbria and southern Scotland – as nearly every weekend we went off in the car, following the lovely byways that abound in that region. My father was careful and courteous in his driving, as in all else he did, but nevertheless we had a serious accident one Saturday afternoon.

We were returning from a picnic on the moors and had collected a fine bunch of heather which would last most of the winter and gladden the heart during the months without flowers. As we climbed a long, steep hill we approached an intersection where the traffic on the other road was completely hidden from view. Our little Austin 7 was going slowly, as indeed it had no choice on the long pull uphill but, just the same, my father sounded the horn before crossing.

Half-way over, a large, powerful car travelling at high speed caught us 'aft amidships', to use my father's nautical terms, spun our car around and threw it some twenty feet to land facing the direction from which we had been coming. The door was broken open and my mother fell to the road while my little sister and I flew through the air with the heather and the picnic basket to come to earth among a group of trees thirty feet away. My father never knew how he left the Austin, he only remembered the shock of seeing the approaching car, switching off the engine and picking my mother up from the road.

Naturally, there were no witnesses. The driver of the large car was a young girl and she was genuinely distressed at the havoc she had caused. My father, ever a gentleman, made the fatal mistake of not accusing her outright, making her responsible for the accident. Perhaps because his own family was thankfully still alive and apparently only shaken, he was reluctant to add to her agitation. The road scout and the policeman from the nearest village who eventually appeared, found all the evidence for assessing blame in the marks on the road and the blood on the forehead of the two passengers sitting in the front seat who had struck the windscreen violently at the moment of impact.

Our car was considerably damaged so we were eventually towed to a village. We put up in a hotel for the night and slept very badly due to the innumerable bruises and the fright. The next day the Austin was loaded on to an empty cattle truck and, with us sitting ignominiously inside the car, returned home.

The subsequent analysis of the accident showed an impressive number of 'ifs'. If we had been travelling faster, we would not have been hit; if our Austin had been a saloon car instead of an open sports model my sister and I would have probably broken our necks against the roof; if we had been hit full amidships instead of slightly aft the car would have overturned and been thoroughly mangled, passengers included; if my sister and I had hit one of those trees among which we landed it would most likely have been fatal; if the girl had been travelling at a reasonable speed she would have been able to brake sufficiently or take evasive action; if my father had not switched off the engine, there might have been a fire, and finally, if my father had formally accused the young lady as being solely responsible for the accident, he would not have received the summons to appear before the County Court on a charge of careless driving.

This incredible derivation shook our law-abiding, peaceful household to its foundations. The County Police, however, had not reckoned with my mother. My father had already gone to work when the summons arrived but she immediately took the first bus to the County town in question and demanded an explanation for this gross miscarriage of justice - British justice! - which was supposed to be a model for the whole civilized world. Who was responsible for this abominable accusation against a fine, careful citizen, when all the evidence pointed to the real culprit even without the need for witnesses? Who was that girl anyway? It seems she was the daughter of a man of position and influence in the County and hence the shameful use of privilege to cover her at the expense of my non-influential father. It was a shock to us then that such a situation could occur in England and I still feel sorry about this breach of faith. There is not even the satisfaction of being able to say that in the end justice was done.

After my mother's visit, the charge against my father was hurriedly dropped and the damages to the car were paid by the girl's insurance company, but she was never charged with careless driving, nor ordered to pay any damages to us. There had been the hotel and transport bills, we had all been severely shaken and lost our picnic gear and the beautiful heather.

My mother had to make several visits to the doctor for over a year because of persistent pain in the spinal column. Apparently something had become dislodged and one day when she tripped over a kerb she felt a 'click' in her back. Whatever it was that had bothered her so long, had slipped fortuitously back into place. That, of course, is not the most efficient way of curing a back injury and had Divine Providence not intervened to make up the lack of medical attention, it may have led to much more serious consequences.

Illnesses were not frequent in my family and we were great believers in simple, wholesome food, fresh air, exercise and the early-to-bed-early-to-rise philosophy. Although not necessarily because of this, we were spared the dreaded illnesses which are now disappearing thanks to the vaccinations and immunizations given to children. Diphtheria, scarlet fever, polio and other dramatic diseases were an ever-present menace but there was no one in our circle of relations and acquaintances who had ever heard of inflammation of the periosteum of the tibia until I contracted it and spent a whole month in bed as a result. It only meant that I had suffered a blow on the knot of muscles at the top of the shin below my kneecap.

I didn't remember any blow in particular among the many that a child receives in the course of normal activities but when my knee swelled up painfully the doctor made me have an X-ray taken and then keep the leg up for four weeks. The knee was painted with iodine every day and I was warned that I really must keep the leg immobile otherwise it could become necessary to amputate it. Such a threat was immediately effective and added an alarming danger to my already noteworthy complaint. In those days, to have an X-ray taken was a sure boost to one's status and in the juvenile jostling for popularity the incidence of this illness and its treatment helped to compensate my mediocre ranking.

Background Data

Some time later, I achieved momentary fame on being bitten by an adder though it should be mentioned that this misfortune provoked considerable incredulity as such accidents seem to be unusual in Britain. The incident took place when my cousin and I were exploring a marshy river bank during a vacation in Bellingham, a country town in Northumberland at the foot of the Cheviot Hills. We were scrambling through the long grasses when I felt a sharp pain on the ankle and thought I had been stung by a wasp. By the time we had returned to the hotel my ankle was greatly swollen and an angry purple hue. We consulted the nearby pharmacist who at once pointed out the two unmistakable marks of the fangs of an adder. Naturally I made the most of such an exotic accident in the everlasting 'oneupmanship' of youngsters.

This desire to be different from the others had its limits. It was acceptable to have been born in another country, in my case Ireland,

'Long ago and faraway'. Author in Belfast 1924

though that could not compare with a schoolfriend who had been born in Palestine and had been to Bethlehem, Nazareth, Galilee and Jerusalem. Or to go to unusual places for vacations, like Auchenshugell, instead of such common resorts as Blackpool, though here again I had another friend who went in successive years to France, Norway and Germany. Or, to take Spanish as a second foreign language instead of the traditional German. The choice of Spanish was greeted with disparaging remarks such as 'What good will that be to you? German would be far more useful' and to tell the truth I don't know why I chose it except that it attracted me in some undefinable way. Even more, I don't know how I was allowed to take it as a subject because other offbeat fancies of mine were unceremoniously squashed.

The desire to be different did not extend to clothes. Preferably clothes had to be inconspicuous from my point of view and durable from my parents' point of view. We used to get a new outfit, hat, coat or suit, gloves and shoes to be inaugurated every Easter Sunday. It may seen rank ingratitude, but those 'Easter Parades' in the new finery were a veritable ordeal. Knowing my family's sober tastes, there must have been little reason for feeling self-conscious but every new hat filled me with horror. It never occurred to me to refuse outright to wear something I didn't like, which is the normal reaction these days and to which I was introduced by my own children.

Some years later, during the unhappy periods of pimples, boils and styes, my mother learned of an infallible cure for these disorders when all the orthodox medications failed to help. In the neighbouring town of Whitley Bay, there was a Mrs. 'X' who prepared a herbal beverage for boil-sufferers and, according to all the enthusiastic testimonies, it was little short of miraculous. As it was necessary to drink this brew immediately after preparation it could never be bottled or swallowed anywhere except on the lady witchdoctor's premises and the complete cure involved drinking a cupful every twenty-one days or so over a period of three to six months. Apart from its undoubted healing powers, the concoction was remarkable for its unspeakable taste. Mrs. 'X' duly warned the patient who was paying a first visit and urged that the dose be downed in one gulp. In spite of being thus forewarned, the taste was a breathtaking shock, so much so that there were some patients who refused to come back to complete the treatment.

Mrs. 'X' would not give any clue as to the recipe apart from the fact that it was a secret herbal remedy handed down for generations in her family and that it contained some stout. She affirmed that she first tasted every fresh brew before administering it to make sure that it was perfect. It was served lukewarm but it seemed to course through the body like an icy stream and immediately after the dose the gasping patient was given a dry biscuit to munch in order to counteract the taste and recover from the shock.

Shortly after I had been through this trial-by-taste for the third time with promising results, my aunt Nan decided she would go too, because of a painful, unyielding carbuncle and naturally enough my mother accompanied her. She gulped down the remedy and promptly fainted. It is not difficult to imagine the consternation in that old-fashioned parlour. My mother remembers exclaiming: 'Mercy on us, it's killed her!' and her anguish mounted up as aunt Nan lay motionless for several minutes.

According to Mrs. 'X' she must have been severely run down, principally due to the carbuncle, because although everyone reacted to the brew with vigorous disgust, no one had ever before been knocked out cold. My mother had visions of police and coroner's inquests and sensational newspaper reports and she must have been ready to faint too. It took us all a long time to get over the emotions and the alarming possibilities and the great mystery has ever since been 'What on earth did that stuff contain?' Perhaps I should clarify that my aunt duly recovered and had no more trouble with carbuncles.

Those difficult years of adolescence and secondary school were strongly marked by friendship with Alison. She was one of a family of seven children, a family unlike all others that I knew and, even now, after so many years and experiences, I still regard it as having been quite out of the ordinary.

Alison's father was a living dynamo, who ran his family, his business and his personal activities with great zest, energy and success and whose generosity to numerous good causes was admirable. It seems to me he could be regarded as the great granddaddy of present-day 'joggers' who are perhaps under the impression that their running exercise is a very up-to-date development. Way back in the twenties and thirties, he could be seen trotting several miles in the early morning to the beach, often taking a dip in the gelid North Sea even in mid-winter and jogging back home before taking the commuter's train to his office. He gave support and funds to local youth and sporting affairs and was also deeply interested and involved in the social problems which affected so many people in those days of the Great Depression.

Every year in August, he took his family *en bloc* for a month to the Lake District where he rented an entire country boarding house, every member of the family inviting along a friend for one or two weeks. To complete the picture, a motor coach or charabanc was hired for the day to transport everyone to Ullswater and, in order to make full use of the coach, other friends and acquaintances were taken there and back as a day's excursion.

Alison invited me as her guest for several years running in the

My friend Alison

Background Data

early thirties and those vacations were unforgettable. To start with, the boarding house was deep in the country, with the added incomparable virtue of being on the shores of Lake Ullswater near the tiny village of Patterdale.

The woods, mountains, streams and gardens made up exactly that sort of countryside in which I longed to live. If there was a flaw in the picture, it was that no horses were included. We were practically always out of doors, working up great country appetites. There was a large rowing boat with two sets of oars and we had some canoes, so the varied contingent of young people and, we might say, young-hearted adults, spent hours on and in the water or exploring the islands and promontories within reach.

One of the promontories was ideal for hide-and-seek and I remember a particular game because I had hidden myself to perfection high up in an old pine. While I sat there astride a branch, keeping absolutely still, a red squirrel appeared on a side branch more or less at eye level. We sat and looked at each other a long time and eventually he jumped away out of sight, leaving me brimming with delight, so much so that I came quickly down the tree to tell the other kids about my great experience, even though it meant losing the game.

No doubt for a city child it was something never to be forgotten, a living page out of one of Beatrix Potter's stories or *The Wind in the Willows*. The red squirrel was, in fact, in those far-off days already quite scarce having almost succumbed in the face of the introduction of the much larger grey American squirrel into Britain.

Obviously 'mountaineering' was another of our most popular activities. The highest mountain in the area was Helvellyn, a mere pimple of some 3,000 feet but perfect as an introduction to the fascinating art of climbing mountains. It was almost a point of honour to go up Helvellyn at least once during the month, and the more enthusiastic and athletic began to set record times for going to the summit and back. Needless to say, I was not one of them.

The first part of the climb was really a long walk upwards through low bush and over springy turf to a high ridge, called Striding Edge, then up the last haul over rocks and screes to the summit. Striding Edge was certainly the most exciting part, a narrow track over a rugged, broken saddle which descended steeply without obstacles on the one side way down to a valley and on the other to a small tarn or lagoon, far below.

We also took long, long walks among the mountains, sometimes to collect blaeberries that grow wild high up on the moors and which are best eaten in tarts. It was inevitable that there would be plenty of rain and we were often soaked and re-soaked in our tramping in the hills or boating on the lake.

One day we added an ambitious ingredient to our mountaineering. The neighbouring farmer was intending to bring down his sheep from the mountain, so Alison's father assured him that 'the boys and girls' would do it for him. We eventually found ourselves posted at different levels on the mountain-side and the idea was to drive all before us. I was soon scrambling behind half a dozen sheep but they suddenly dropped from sight down a very loose scree and I slithered and staggered after them. By the time I reached firm ground they had disappeared into the scrub and after making some futile efforts to locate them, I had to give up. I found I had descended to the woods bordering the lake so the only thing to do was to tramp back to the boarding house. Hours later the other amateur shepherds arrived, having delivered twenty-five sheep to the farmer. The fact that there were still another fifty on the mountain did not affect their elation over such an achievement but I had to suffer obvious jokes about Bo-Peep.

How difficult to snap back into urban reality, school work and household chores! Even the facility of having electricity once more was not duly appreciated. The oil lamps and candles had seemed so appropriate.

Alison's house was also a source of wonderment to me, although outwardly it was just one of a terrace of huge, antiquated Victorian residences with numerous outsize, high-ceilinged rooms that would require an army of servants for their upkeep. They were built for the large middle-class families of the era that ended with World War I, though many of those houses still exist and, by now, most have been converted into self-contained apartments and adapted according to modern standards of comfort. It is not surprising that this particular house attracted me so much but if I had been asked in those days what I liked most about it, I would have answered unhesitatingly 'The bannister!' This was smooth and sturdy and ran uninterrupted from the attics down three storeys to the hall on the ground floor - a perfect slide, well-polished from countless descents by presumably many generations of children.

Yet another feature distinguishing this family from humdrum, ordinary folk like ourselves, was the fact that Alison's father had been married first to a Russian lady with whom he had three daughters. She had died suddenly and in due course he married again, so that there was a considerable distance between the first three and the next four children. I did not often see the older daughters, who were already launched on their careers or marriages but, perhaps partly because of their exotic Russian mother, I thought they were perfectly lovely, so elegant and poised, light-years away from my clumsy, overweight self.

One year, in fact the last of the visits to Ullswater, Alison and I went on a great adventure alone. We sailed on a coastal steamer from the Tyne to Aberdeen and then cycled across Scotland to the English Lake District, a journey of 250 miles. In Aberdeen, Stirling and Glasgow we stayed a couple of days with relations but in between we used Youth Hostels which were located at very convenient distances for a day's cycling. I imagine our unaccompanied tour must have caused some raised eyebrows among relatives and friends and maybe our parents suffered doubts and fears at such premature independence. Our arrival at Ullswater was celebrated as a great achievement but two weeks later I had to cycle home alone right across the north of England. It was quite an ordeal as the road follows the ancient Roman Wall which, of course, means going straight across the countryside, up hill and down dale instead of rambling English-style around the contours. Presumably I walked nearly half the journey.

About a year later World War II began and another era ended. Gradually, much of the population was dispersed to different activities all connected with the war effort. I joined the Civil Service in another part of the country and Alison enlisted in the Women's Royal Naval Service. Prior to being sent abroad, she was given the usual inoculations against tropical diseases but something went wrong, for she died of meningitis at the age of 21. In the midst of the daily tragedies of wartime, this was for me the saddest of all.

In dwelling on these recollections of friendship, I realize regretfully that there never was a close relationship with my only sister, Winifred. Perhaps the three and a half year difference in age was too much in our early years and meant that we had different groups of friends and interests. She did not share any of my obsessions, she was brilliant at school. In addition, she was very sensitive and when we quarrelled frequently in true sisterly fashion, it seemed to me that I was always to blame: 'I should have known better since I was so much older', which was very probably true. When the war broke out I was seventeen and Win thirteen and I left home to work in the 'war effort'. By the end of the war I was getting ready to go to Argentina while she was about to go to Switzerland on a University exchange scholarship. Curiously, we both eventually settled down respectively in these widely-separated countries and only sporadically have we been able to get together.

Another constant companion of childhood was my cousin Colin, who lived not far away from us. He was about my age and, looking back, I suppose he was more like a brother than a cousin. We made experiments with his chemistry set, swapped stamps, played spy games and made war with his lead soldiers. In the brief, cool summers when the families went to spend the day on the beach, we explored rockpools for crabs and sea anemones and bathed in the uninviting North Sea waves until overcome with shivering.

Poor Colin, who was slight of build compared to our more robust family, would be almost blue when he emerged from the sea, but he was as strong and athletic as most other boys of his own age. He was an enthusiastic Boy Scout and this was a bond of sympathy with my activities in the Girl Guides.

Early in World War II Colin joined the Royal Air Force and became a bomber pilot. I could never imagine him handling a large aircraft, dodging enemy flak and fighter planes, dropping bombs and facing the innumerable hazards of aerial warfare. He went out on twenty-two successful operations but he never returned from the twenty-third. Although this was no surprise it was nonetheless heartbreaking. I still feel a lump in my throat when I think of him, a prototype of all the other young men whose death overshadowed the years that followed.

Background Data

The Boy Scout and Girl Guide organizations of those days were an important part of life. Along with many of my friends I joined the Guides at age 7 as a Brownie, and continued right up to the Rangers on becoming 16 years old. The companionship, games, camps, the ideals of the Scouting movement were, I think, a very valuable factor in helping along the difficult years of adolescence and I regretted many times that in Argentina there were no Girl Guides for my daughters. Scouts, or similar organizations, existed – and exist – for boys, though it would appear that the military connotations of uniforms and ranks make them slightly suspect from the viewpoint of large portions of the population who have no love for the military system. As for Guides, they just fit nowhere into the picture, although I do know that one Company existed in the northern suburbs of Buenos Aires. At this stage of the game it seems unlikely that Guiding will ever become installed in Argentina, perhaps because things that were important once, no longer are so for new generations in new surroundings.

While recalling our activities with the Scouts and Guides, I looked up Baden-Powell's *Scouting for Boys*, first published in 1908, my copy being the 1960 edition. The index alone gives a very good idea of the vast scope of the apparently simple principles of Scouting, the Movement having been described by a former President of the Board of Education as 'one of the happiest of educational discoveries'. However, from all one sees and hears about youth today, I imagine that some of Baden-Powell's 'homilies' would perhaps be incomprehensible: chivalry, patriotism, service to others, obedience, courtesy, honesty, clean living, love and understanding of Nature, kindness to animals, cheerfulness and other old-fashioned virtues. One wonders how much has been lost. It is to be hoped the Scout Movement will continue to play its unique rôle in finding congenial solutions to the conflicts and difficulties which afflict young people today.

2

Over the Sea to Argentina

The Second World War was been dealt with thoroughly from all possible angles and is still the subject of books and films. My contribution was un-exciting and made no headlines. I worked as temporary Civil Servant from 1940-1945 in a Ministry far from the danger areas, and had no more harrowing experiences or perilous encounters than I might have had in peacetime. At one time I volunteered for service abroad and towards the end of 1945 when hostilities had ceased I found myself on the way to a post in Buenos Aires.

There were no direct services between England and Argentina at that precise moment so it was decided I should go first to New York where onward transport would be arranged.

The journey began by battling for ten days across a furious Atlantic Ocean in an old banana boat. Most of the passengers were war brides and their babies and it is easy to imagine the poor seasick mothers wished they were dead. Diapers festooned the rails of the passageways and the wailing of infants often rose above the noise of the storm. Off Labrador the storms ceased and we entered an eerie blanket of thick fog which covered us practically as far as Halifax.

Canada lay deep in snow and the wide, white landscape which unfolded on the train journey from Halifax to New York confirmed our traditional romantic impression that winters in Canada were wonderful. At one point the train stopped for half an hour at a town whose name I forget but which is otherwise memorable because there

Over the Sea to Argentina

in a fruitstore close to the station we bought an entire stalk of bananas – the first we had seen for six years. In England bananas had been one of the early 'casualties' of the war being classified as an unnecessary import. We must have seemed rather childish in our delight.

It was eight o'clock on a Sunday morning when the train reached New York and the groups of travelling companions that had formed in the previous two weeks dispersed, presumably for ever. I had one dollar left from the miserable allowance of twelve pounds sterling which could be taken out of England at that time. There was no one to meet me at the station but the dollar was enough to pay for a taxi to the hotel where I had a conditional reservation.

At the reception desk the girl said the hotel was full but that they would put an extra cot in a room which I would have to share with another woman. I wondered what good a cot would be to me, as up to that moment the word 'cot' had always meant a baby's bed and I did not realize it was in the same category as 'elevator' and 'lift'. It was the first of several language differences which cropped up in the next few days.

On the Monday I made the necessary arrangements for continuing my journey to Buenos Aires and with a hundred dollars advance, I joyously began to replace my war-weary clothes. During the war all clothing had been rationed with a system of coupons. The coupon allowance was very meagre and meant that clothes were patched and darned and modified until they practically fell apart. As shoes, overcoats, suits and dresses required many coupons, we were loathe to use the precious tokens on underwear so it is not difficult to imagine that little remained of the original garments after the endless mending and re-mending. The purchase of new underwear in New York therefore had first priority and I happily ditched my last relics of austerity in the waste basket of the hotel room, not without some misgivings about what the maid would think of the discarded rags.

The next purchase was a pair of shoes and after wandering down Fifth Avenue for a while I noticed a likely pair. The salesman, when he saw the shoes I was wearing looked shocked. They were good solid utility brogues and had lasted me two years through the worst trials of the English weather and numerous repairs. 'Are you from England?'

he asked, 'Only English women would wear shoes like that.'

I suppose I said something about having been through the war and rationing because he quickly became anxious to help me wipe out my dreadful memories and find a decent pair of shoes. It did not take long to chose a pair, which I can remember in detail: supple dark-blue leather, medium heels, elegant simple style and light but strong soles. I still think of them as the nicest shoes I ever had but that opinion may be partly influenced by the contrast between the old serviceable clodhoppers and the more feminine style so many times postponed until then.

Those few days in New York were evidently devoted to the materialistic pursuit of the clothes and food that had been denied to us during the war years. It was like a dream to be free of ration cards and coupons and to be limited only by the conditions of one's purse. In retrospect I look upon this my only visit to the U.S. as sadly marred by undue preoccupations with creature comforts when I should have been taking the opportunity to visit as many interesting places as possible. I was living in a sort of vacuum and once or twice in some New York street I found myself thinking, 'What am I doing here? There must be some mistake.'

The trip was being handled by people I never knew or saw and although my destination was Buenos Aires, I had no idea what to expect there and so far no one had been able to enlighten me. The general impression was that it was very hot and was also a dangerous place for women. From New York I had to go to Miami by train and then by air to Rio de Janeiro where I would have to wait for a connection to Buenos Aires.

In those early post-war days, long distance travel was difficult to arrange and was subject to many delays and cancellations. The Silver Arrow from New York to Miami was like no train I had ever travelled in before, including prior to the war. As had happened in New York, so again I allowed myself to be impressed by the comfort and efficiency available to the traveller instead of observing the numerous famous and interesting places along the route.

With memories still fresh in the mind of the rigorous, depressing experience of travelling in a cold, unlit train, often standing for hours in a crowded passageway, with departure and arrival times subject to unannounced modifications, sometimes waiting hopelessly on a bleak unknown station for a connection, it is perhaps not surprising that I was in such an unspiritual frame of mind. The club car with its bar, scattered lounge chairs and big observation windows seemed the inspiration of a genius, while the ladies' Powder Room was the work of an even greater genius, starting with its very name and including the generous dimensions, the ample mirrors, the easy chairs, the carpet on the floor, the ice-water fountain, the hot and cold water in the several washbasins and the perfectly functioning plumbing throughout. Even in peacetime the British trains had never offered such an accumulation of refinements.

Miami was the springboard for diving into the really unknown. It was also the introduction to the unfamiliar because until then the U.S. had not seemed to be a 'foreign' country, presumably because of the many cultural links with Britain and a superficial familiarity with American Life acquired through the cinema. Here it was different.

December in Miami was warm and sunny, palm trees lined the avenues, tall white buildings rose along the seaboard, and the notices in the hotel were in English and Spanish. If in New York I had been concentrating on food and clothes, here in Miami I was faced with a hitherto minor problem which incredibly proved insoluble and prevented me from making the most of two days in Florida. A painful stye appeared on my eyelid and I went to look for a pharmacy to buy the remedy which had always previously been effective. The pharmacy was of course a drugstore and medicines seemed to be the least important branch of the business. I asked for boracic lint and the word 'lint' proved to be unknown in any medical connection. Even when I described it, no recognition was forthcoming and I went away disconsolate with a packet of cotton wool and a recommended lotion. The wretched stye therefore began to run its painful course and that's about all I remember of Miami.

The stye also deadened the excitement of taking off on my first flight ever in an aeroplane and when I asked the steward if he had some lint or other remedy for my eye he shook his head. He was very sympathetic but explained that there was no first-aid kit on board so all he could offer were some paper handkerchiefs. It seemed odd there was no first-aid kit in the plane. I wondered whether the theory

Where The Devil Lost His Poncho

was that if the plane should crash no one would need first-aid or anything else any more.

The plane was a DC-3, the great aviation work-horse of the 1940s and 1950s. It cruised smoothly over the lovely Caribbean, awash with changing colours and speckled with fluffy clouds.

It was understood the first stopover would be Trinidad but we came down in Santo Domingo, at the time known as Ciudad Trujillo after the dictator then in power. We were told we would be spending the night there because the pilot had an important date. Nowadays that would presumably be considered a rather light-hearted way to run an airline. Nobody seemed to mind, however, and after checking in at a comfortable Miami-style hotel, we went shopping and sightseeing. Since by then my eye was practically closed, much of the fascination of this pretty town was lost on me. The British Representative invited a group of us to his apartment for drinks in the evening and he and his wife were so charming and entertaining that I almost forgot my misery.

The next day we were airborne at dawn and heading for Pará-Belen in Brazil, via Trinidad. At Trinidad we had over an hour's wait and most of the passengers went to look around the town. I was the only one with a British passport and as Trinidad was then a British colony I had expected to be first through the Customs. I was asked to wait a minute for some bureaucratic reason and the minute became so prolonged that in the end there was no time to go anywhere. The American passengers were very amused at this minor outrage but perhaps my gummed-up eye had worried the Customs men and they had thought it would be better to keep me in the airport. During the next leg of the flight we met some enormous cloud formations, with the consequent stomach-dropping turbulence. I was very proud of myself at not being sick and in fact I was more impressed by the terrible green hue of the face of a passenger across the gangway.

The flight seemed interminable over the tightly packed jungle and eventually in the inky blackness of the night a tiny square of lights appeared, the airport of Pará-Belen. As soon as the plane stopped, some men in white coats rushed in and shoved a thermometer in everybody's mouth. This really alarmed me as the stye on my eye was at its maximum repulsiveness and it would not have surprised me if I had had a raging temperature to match. Apparently I was still healthy enough to enter the country and after a long taxi trip through utter darkness we reached the hotel for the night.

I was shown into a vast old-fashioned room and for the first time since leaving home I regretted my bold step into the unknown. Even so late at night the heat was asphyxiating, there were unidentified insects flying and crawling about, the bed somehow didn't look inviting and the pain in my eye refused to relent. Maybe I would have fallen asleep with exhaustion if something had not run across the room just as I was dozing off and that decided me. I collected my belongings, told the desk clerk I would not be using the room any more and went to the lounge for the rest of the night. Here I was introduced to coffee as it is drunk in the country so closely associated with it and it was a revelation. All the coffee I had ever drunk until that moment evidently bore no relation whatever to the Real Thing.

The next day we were no sooner aloft when I fell soundly asleep. On awaking I could only open one eye because the stye had finally run its course and burst of its own accord. The steward brought me warm water and some more paper handkerchiefs to clean up the mess and I arrived at Rio de Janeiro feeling like a new person.

Rio de Janeiro is without doubt a place that everyone should see. It is dramatically beautiful from the air, from the harbour, at dawn, at sunset, at night. It was my great good fortune to have to wait eight days for a connection to Buenos Aires and I stayed with an Anglo-Brazilian family in Copacabana, who lived close to the famous beach. When it was time to leave for Buenos Aires I wondered how I would ever settle down again to working the daily grind.

It was December, the beginning of summer in Buenos Aires. Just as people had said, it was intensely hot and it was only six months later in the following May when the Southern Hemisphere winter was approaching that I regretted having so light-heartedly given away most of my heavy clothing before leaving England.

I should have written down my first impressions of Argentina as soon as I arrived, because fifty years later it is difficult to recall just what made the most impact. It was mid-December and very hot when I landed at the old international airport called Morón. That did not strike me as a nice name for a place, though in fact it means in

Spanish a hillock or mound. I was met at the airport to my great relief and after a seemingly interminable journey in glare and dust, I was deposited in the apartment where I was to stay until I found my own permanent lodgings. The apartment was deliciously cool and quiet even though it was in the centre of the city. There was a bowl of jasmines on the night-table and I thought they had a most beautiful fragrance. After a while, however, I had to put the bowl on the balcony because the tropical perfume was overpowering.

I was trying hard to adjust to the idea of starting to work the next day. It had been only too easy to adjust to travelling from one exotic place to another and the journey had turned out to be so long and interesting that the thought of sitting down in an office and typing for three years was thoroughly depressing.

The next evening I was invited out for my first Argentine dinner and was introduced to the biggest, tenderest steaks in the world, followed by meringue with Chantilly cream. I recall this meringue because when I ordered it I anticipated something the size of a tennis ball, for instance, as remembered from pre-war days in England. This Argentine meringue was the size of an ostrich egg and had so much cream I was ashamed of myself for having ordered it.

As time went on I grew accustomed to this abundance of food but there was always the nagging thought that back in England food remained rationed while on the Continent of Europe, famine was never very far away. I tried to pacify my conscience by sending regular food parcels home and my family was very pleased to receive them, though sometimes they wondered: what on earth . . .?

There is a very special product here called *dulce de leche* and anyone with just a Spanish-English dictionary could be forgiven for guessing it would mean sweetened milk. It is, however, literally milk jam and it is the colour of caramel. It is truly delicious and I have often thought it would be a great success in England and the U.S. The English have fame as being very sweet-toothed and the world's greatest consumers of candies and chocolate, so they would probably relish it. *Dulce de leche* is often used in cakes and desserts instead of cream, spread on bread or biscuits or, when the children figure no one is looking, in large spoonfuls.

There is also a kind of *dulce* or jam which is eaten with cheddar or cream cheese. The two usual varieties of the jam are sweet potato and quince and they come in solid form to be cut into portions along with slices of cheese. This cheese and jam (or *queso y dulce*) is known as the Policeman's Dessert, but I still have to find out why. I once sent a tin of sweet potato jam in a food parcel and the family debated a long time over what it was. They had already had a slight shock on a previous occasion when they opened a tin of *dulce de leche*, thinking it would be some sort of white condensed milk to serve along with a can of Argentine peaches. The caramel colour suggested the milk had deteriorated en route but in the end they tried it and decided it was food for the gods. On the whole, however, the parcels were made up of well-known articles such as rice, butter, powdered eggs, sugar, coffee and canned fruit.

Another permanently remembered first impression was the heat of Buenos Aires in the summer. Air conditioning in those days seemed confined to the cinemas and very new buildings, otherwise one resorted to fans, iced drinks and a minimum of activity. Just to blink one's eyelids caused the perspiration to pour down the face and often the high temperatures continue through the night. In the centre of the city many streets are narrow, the heat remains trapped between the high buildings and, combined with the normally high level of humidity, Buenos Aires is a Turkish bath rather than a furnace. In March and April, the heat begins to ease off and the autumn is, like spring, very agreeable.

About my first winter in Argentina, I can only remember regretting having come unprepared for the cold days. In comparison with England, the Buenos Aires winter is negligible. In June, July and August, one can expect rain, cold days, a few frosts, some warm periods and a general longing for the spring and summer.

Thunderstorms are a feature of the hot weather and guaranteed to cause a lasting impression. The build-up is almost theatrical: oppressive heat, utterly still air, ominous darkening of the sky by tremendous black clouds, brilliant flashes of lightning north, south, east and west, and the growling of the thunder increasing in intensity. Soon a few large drops of rain splash down and sizzle on the hot pavements, followed by the deluge with full orchestration of blinding, continuous lightning from all directions and appalling crashes of thunder. The fury of the rain is unbelievable and anyone could be forgiven for thinking the end of the world must be near. The storms often last many hours, cause considerable damage and flooding but they bring a few days' relief from the suffocating heat until the next build-up.

Buenos Aires appears to be situated at the point where the great masses of hot air from the tropics meet the cold air from the Antarctic, hence the violence of the collision. These highly spectacular storms occur mostly in summer but a curious phenomenon invariably takes place near the end of winter around 30 August, known as the Santa Rosa storm. This is the date of the feast of Santa Rosa, patron saint of the Americas. She was born in Lima, Perú, in 1586 and was the first saint born and raised in the New World. Her gentle, holy life would seem totally unconnected with any kind of violence.

A few weeks' residence in Argentina was enough to evoke surprise at some history which had hitherto passed unmentioned in our textbooks in England.

In 1812 a British army landed on the shores of the River Plate, captured Buenos Aires city and soon after was ignominiously thrown out and routed. This is known as the Reconquista, or Reconquest. It is celebrated on 12 August. The captured British banners and flags are preserved in one of the old churches and the holes made by the cannon fire are still there on the church walls for all the world to see.

I was astounded to learn, not that the British troops had been beaten by a sort of citizens' army but the fact that this was the first time I had heard about the expedition. History had been one of my stronger points at school, thanks to the enthusiasm of our teacher who knew how to transmit his own profound knowledge and love of his subject to an unwilling class of students determined from the start to be bored with history.

The importance of the Reconquista was second only to the problem of the Islas Malvinas or Falklands. That there were Falkland Islands somewhere in the world, I knew from my stamp album. Maybe I knew they were in the South Atlantic but that they had any connection with Argentina was a genuine surprise. Presumably, it was also a surprise to the British in general in 1982, who I understand were mostly unaware of the existence and location of the Falklands.

Over the Sea to Argentina

Times have changed greatly since 1945 and the proud British Lion has been sadly diminished in power and prestige but to anyone like myself reared in the assumption that British is Best in all things material and spiritual, I was being exposed to the uncomfortable process of 'seeing ourselves as other see us'. It was difficult to accept that the British would gloss over or ignore their own past humiliations or that they would wrongfully take over someone else's territories or in fact that they would willingly or knowingly be beastly in any way.

Since it is now obvious that the British always had their full share of human frailties and that they have become resigned to relinquishing their imperial status, it is curious how their passions were aroused with such bellicose fury over the Argentine attempt to recover her long-lost islands. A look at the map should be enough to convince anyone that all connections with Great Britain no longer make any sense but perhaps the reaction was so violent because they represented the last vestiges of a once-proud empire. They were taken by force from Argentina in 1833 and the wound never healed. For Argentina, the Malvinas are her lost daughter, stolen by a foreign kidnapper, who made her change her name and her sentiments and who, at the same time, kept her in melancholy isolation, a second-class citizen, to labour for a commercial company which would reap most of the benefits and own most of the land.

It is certainly a tragedy that the Argentine military dictatorship broke away from the long drawn out diplomatic negotiations which seemed so unfruitful but had yet made some progress. The military government, having failed on all civilian fronts and knowing that public opinion would rejoice unanimously over the recovery of the Malvinas, played its last card, only to show serious incompetence in its own specific military sphere.

The excruciating pain of defeat seared the very soul of the nation, but the defeat helped to bring back democracy and the Constitution. If the military had managed to keep the islands, it would probably have been a long, difficult task to remove the dictators from power. The pain and anguish over the islands, however, will not diminish and, meanwhile, real friendship between Britain and Argentina is problematic. Very many Argentines have family ties with the British Isles. Large numbers of English, Scots, Welsh and Irish made their homes in Argentina from its earliest years as an independent nation and many have prospered greatly.

It is calculated that ten to fifteen thousand Irish immigrants reached Argentina during the nineteenth century, especially after 1840, as hunger and poverty became ever more crushing in Ireland. Most of them settled in the province of Buenos Aires as shepherds and farmers and played an early, decisive rôle in the development of the agrarian structure and the rural 'petite bourgeoisie' of the Province. Naturally, not all became wealthy ranchers but the assimilation of the Irish into their new surroundings was extraordinary. In January 1875, the English-language Catholic newspaper, *The Southern Cross*, published in Buenos Aires wrote: 'In no part of the world is the Irishman more respected and esteemed than in the Province of Buenos Aires; and in no part of the world, in the same space of time, have Irish settlers made such large fortunes.'

Among the Irish who became famous here is William Brown, born in Cork in 1777. He came to Argentina as a member of the British Navy at the time of Argentina's struggle for independence. Adventurous and daring he organized a naval force for Argentina and led it through a series of spectacular victories against the Spanish. Thus he became Almirante Guillermo Brown, the founding father of the Argentine Navy, which he again conducted successfully through crucial battles in the early nineteenth-century war against the Brazilian Empire. He died in Buenos Aires in 1857 and is to this day regarded with genuine reverence.

It is a pleasure to recall that my first friends in Argentina were members of the Irish community. They were warmly hospitable and helpful in my new ambience, strikingly different from the Anglo-Argentine community which maintained a rigid caste system among its members and a Pukka Sahib disdain for the 'natives'.

The English seem to require at least three generations to become assimilated. Many born locally and who had never visited England or whose grandparents had been English, would talk about England as 'home' or refer to 'our' king, for example. They talked loudly in English on buses and trains and some were even proud that they could not speak Spanish. During my first days in Buenos Aires I was introduced to an Anglo-Argentine lady who was greatly distressed over a family tragedy: her daughter was going to marry an Argentine! I suggested that it appeared a normal sort of situation, living in Argentina, which, of course, immediately caused her to regard me as disloyal.

There were several 'posh' English schools, run on pseudo-Eton lines and some probably costing even more in fees, and one of their perennial difficulties concerned the Malvinas-Falklands Islands. The bilingual schools in Argentina – British, German, French, Jewish and so on – are obliged to give the local curriculum in the morning, while in the afternoon, subjects are taught in the corresponding foreign language. English geography and history classes therefore encountered the dilemma of ownership of the Islands. Apparently the children saw no problem and on being questioned, would answer: 'In the morning the Islands belong to Argentina and in the afternoon to England.' I suppose that would not be a suitable international solution but it has its childlike beauty.

The English-speaking community has long been well served by its daily newspaper *The Buenos Aires Herald*. In times of repression and censorship, it was very skilful in handling the English language so that news and opinions could get through, perhaps obliquely, to its readers while baffling the censors. The dictatorship from 1976-1982 had the *Herald* on its black list and there were some severe clashes, its reporters and staff being in real danger. The newspaper was recognized everywhere, in Argentina and abroad, as a valiant defender of freedom and human rights. Long before those tragic times and strictly among the community, one of the favourite columns was written periodically by 'B.T.' It was in the form of letters in English by an imaginary Argentine would-be playboy called Ramón, who translated literally from current Argentine Spanish with plenty of everyday slang. It is a pity that enjoyment of its hilarious humour is restricted to a small audience, well acquainted with the Argentine vernacular and having a thorough knowledge of English.

Welsh immigration to Argentina is a dramatic story, a nineteenth-century saga. A group of families, equipped with implements for different trades reached the estuary of the River Chubut in Patagonia in 1865, aboard the sailing ship *Mimosa*. Their first years were extremely harsh and it was mainly thanks to the local Indian Tehuelche tribes that they were able to learn survival in this wild, lonely land. The valley of the River Chubut, however, has flourished and is famed for its farms, its Welsh cakes and cheeses and its towns with strange names like Madryn, Trelew, Trevelin, Gaiman and, of course, with families called Jones, Hughes, Powell, Williams, Evans and Llewellyn.

Sadly, the struggle to keep alive the Welsh language and songs is regarded as practically hopeless as the original Welsh, now long integrated into the Argentine scene, were never renewed by later immigrants. The Argentines as a whole perhaps do not realize how much they are beholden to the small colony that farmed the valley right up to the Andes. At the time of the settling of limits between Argentine and Chile at the beginning of the century, the mountain area was in dispute, so that the British arbitrator called for a plebiscite among the mostly Welsh settlers, in the year 1902, and they were to decide whether they considered themselves Argentines or Chileans. The vote was overwhelmingly in favour of Argentina and Chile accepted the decision without further discussion.

Naturally, the Scots also came to Argentina and their descendants are to be found all over the country. Perhaps some of the most notable achievements of Scots immigrants involved immense sheep-farms in the far south. This demanded the toughness, frugality and undauntedness associated with the Scots as a race, and certainly not many others tried to emulate them, even though the rewards were eventually very substantial.

One of the Scotsmen who became most famous and whose connections with Argentina are still regarded with affection was Robert Cunningham-Grahame, known locally as Don Roberto. Only recently yet another anthology of his writings was published in Buenos Aires and a few years before, the Argentine author, Alicia Jurado, wrote a first-rate biography of him entitled *El Escocés Errante*. This title suggests the key to his personality, a sort of Knight Errant, a nineteenth-century Don Quixote. The preface he wrote to the book by his close friend A.F. Tschiffely, reveals his love of horses and of the great open spaces that abound in Argentina.

Throughout Patagonia, the sheep farms mentioned above which were owned or managed by British interests after the settling of the

'Indian Question' by force of arms, had undoubtedly benefitted as regards their most advantageous location from the information provided by Captain George Chatworth Musters in his book, *At Home with the Patagonians: A Year's Wanderings over Untrodden Ground from the Straits of Magellan to the Rio Negro*, published in 1871. It was the first systematic report on the interior of Patagonia, which had been explored and surveyed thoroughly only along the coasts since it was first visited in 1520 by Magellan.

Musters, a captain in the British Navy, led an adventurous life of exploration and was ever ready to undertake new, daring expeditions. In this particular case he obtained permission from the Tehuelche Indian tribes to travel with them on the annual journey from the southernmost end of the continent to the north of Patagonia, in order to hunt over new ground and replenish their supplies at the end of winter. He became one of them, sharing all their customs and activities and, at the same time, he took note of the places en route which could become 'oases' for settlements in the mostly desolate steppes of southern Argentina. It is surely no coincidence that eventually the favourable locations mentioned by Musters in his fascinating book became the sites of British-owned ranches and establishments that operated very profitably for many decades.

Another colourful component of the Argentine ethnic tapestry corresponds to the Syrian-Lebanese community, known locally as *turcos*. The Argentines were never particularly accurate about the geographical origins of some immigrant groups, *turcos* referring to Arabs in general, while Russians and other Slavs are known as *polacos* and Jews as *rusos*. Immigrants from Spain are lumped together as *gallegos* (Galicians) whether they come from Galicia, Valencia, Andalucia or the other Spanish provinces.

Some of the early *turcos* in Argentina started making a livelihood by travelling with wagon-loads of all kinds of merchandise over great distances throughout the length and breadth of the hinterland, venturing where many others feared to tread. They sold or bartered their provisions in outlying homesteads and small townships, returning to base with wool, furs and other country products. It was a hard existence, of constant exposure to the rigours of climate and terrain, of long, lonely journeys and few comforts. No doubt, this incessant toil became the basis of many a prosperous business in subsequent years.

It was often held against the *turcos* that they gave only a fraction of the value of the goods they brought back and sold profitably in the cities. But in fact they helped link up the dispersed population, bringing news and information along with the goods. Often they took sick or injured persons in their wagons to a doctor, perhaps two days' journey away, like Good Samaritans. Nowadays there are still isolated homesteads and there are still *turcos* who do the rounds but they have stations wagons or trucks and the roads are no longer mere tracks. Even with radio and television to keep up to date on events, the visit of these hardy merchants is a welcome break in the daily routine.

The Arab community never appeared to have a problem of co-existing with the very large Jewish community in Argentina, which has its own particular history of integration into the local scene. Some of the earliest immigrants came fleeing from pogroms in Russia and created successful agricultural colonies in the Mesopotamian region, complete with their own Jewish gauchos and villages such as Moisesville. However, like rural areas everywhere, the drift to urban centres in recent decades has left mostly memories of these once flourishing activities.

There is no evident friction between groups which are antagonistic back in Europe and elsewhere and, from personal observation, I would say that South America as a whole incorporates its newcomers without great difficulty. One of the reasons could be that the children of immigrants born in each land automatically receive the nationality (*jus solis*) thus fostering loyalty and affection for the new homeland.

Only recently I learned, not without some surprise, about the arrival of groups of Boers from South Africa at the beginning of the century. After the Anglo-Boer war in that country, some of the defeated Boers decided to emigrate rather than suffer the humiliation of submitting to the victorious British and endure the difficult post-war economic depression. They decided that their best option was to establish a colony in Argentina, specifically in the Province of Chubut, as farmers and sheep ranchers.

This little-known history is given in a charming book by Johanna Kokot de Avila, *Extraños Injertos en el Arbol Patagónico*, published in Buenos Aires in 1991 and it relates the vicissitudes and accomplishments of the South Africans, whom she describes graphically as 'strange grafts on to the Patagonian tree'. Johanna Kokok was born in 1907 in the pioneer Boer colony of Chubut, near the city of Comodoro Rivadavia, where many of her descendants and those of the other immigrants are the visible evidence that the 'strange grafts' prospered very well on the Patagonian tree.

Another unfamiliar detail of Argentine history is that the earliest settlers in Tierra del Fuego came from the Malvinas, initiating sheep farming on a serious scale in the far south of the country. In the Malvinas it was practically impossible to acquire land and it would support only one and a half sheep per hectare, so Tierra del Fuego and the southernmost provinces exerted a strong attraction on the islanders.

So we come back to the dispute between Argentina and Britain over the Islands which must be solved some day. It is a totally anachronic dispute, a source of dismay to the many Argentines of British descent and others who admired the undoubted qualities inherent in the British tradition illustrated, for instance, by the local phrase *palabra de inglés* meaning word of honour. I must admit this is not heard any more. The nineteenth-century flavour of Empire and Glory in the British attitude to the conflict is so exasperating at this period on the threshold of the twenty-first century, that a generous reaction on both sides is urgent and necessary.

3

Work and Worship

For most of my first thirty-five years in Argentina I worked as a secretary. This may be an activity doomed to extinction, a casualty of the advance of technology, like the fore-and-aft rigged schooner or the horse-drawn carriage. The technological point of no return has probably been passed, if we are to believe Alvin Toffler in his book, *The Third Wave*, so maybe it would be appropriate to recall some experiences as secretary and give the sociologists and historians of the twenty-first century a first-hand account of a twentieth-century institution which once seemed indispensable.

The situation in places like Argentina was particularly interesting for any bilingual secretary and perhaps the local English-speaking women had the greatest amount of opportunities for this work. British interests in Argentina were particularly important until after the Second World War and then American business moved in to fill the gap left by the diminishing British investment. This meant even more openings for the English-Spanish secretary, who only had to become accustomed to American use, or misuse, of the language.

I was at one time secretary to the Vice-President of a famous American corporation's Buenos Aires subsidiary. He believed very strongly that it was only proper to follow American custom in the firm's English correspondence. One of the words that bothered him was 'programme'. Apparently, the only place that 'programme' is seen in the U.S. is on the advertisements for burlesque shows, so it had to be spelled 'program' in case headquarters thought he had developed frivolous ideas. The first time he dictated a letter to me he referred to a 'toob'. When I asked him what that was, he said, 'A toob? Why, a toob – t, u, b, e'. In the course of time I built up a double vocabulary, such as spanner for English and wrench for American, tap and faucet, bumper and fender, puncture and flat, sleeper and tie, and so on in addition to the other more well-known varieties like lift and elevator or petrol and gasoline. It seemed to be my destiny to work among engineers and chemists so the normal difficulties of translation were aggravated by knowing little about the subject itself.

One such job involved a considerable amount of technical translation. The firm was a small Argentine company which worked at high pressure, successfully and informally, the driving genius being an engineer from Central Europe whose bad temper and bad heart were part of the Company folklore. He could converse in half a dozen languages but the correspondence which he dictated in rapid English or Spanish required a sharp ear, imagination and merciless editing. Presumably, he had never learned English in any orthodox way and on his constant trips to the U.S. and Europe he picked up the latest slang expressions and fashionable words.

I had to risk being firm with him and insist on changing them for more sedate language. He would call me an old-fashioned Limey and ask me what I knew about locomotives anyway. Anything which displeased him was 'disgustipating'. I think even the late H.W. Fowler would have approved a motion for the inclusion of this expressive word in the English language.

His bad heart really was a disturbing feature of life in that company. He would be discussing some business or dictating a letter and suddenly he would stop, his face ashen. Falling back in his chair, he would fumble for the drawer where he kept his *remedio*, so whoever was with him had to grab a glass of water and help him take his lifesaving pills. In about five minutes he would recover and sit up sharply, plunging back into the theme where he had left off so dramatically. His senior staff member, who bore the brunt of the Old Man's temper and tantrums and often stayed late at night with him thrashing over problems in the work, once complained darkly: 'The old bastard's going to drop dead here one night when I'm all alone with him and I'll be accused of murder.' I don't know how a computer would handle such situations but along with computer-secretaries, bosses with cardiac disorder are by now presumably using transplants.

Apart from the bilingual aspect of the Argentine scene, the secretary's work was, and will be until she vanishes from the approaching electronic scene, a vital cog in the commercial and industrial wheel. The basic equipment was spelling, grammar, shorthand and typewriting. All the rest depended on the boss. He might expect her to use a slide rule (do they still exist?), compose letters and reports, call up his or his wife's friends to co-ordinate a bridge party or a night at the opera, arrange for a hunting trip to Chile, find out why the main water pipe burst, sew on a button or wipe the egg off his tie, cover up for his sins of omission and commission, invent a filing system, or get someone to go to his house and have a look at the bathroom faucet (tap). It is, therefore, obvious that a secretary required various abstract qualities which could not be taught in a special course or bought in easy instalments and which have not yet been built into computers: resourcefulness, adaptability, serenity, cheerfulness, tact, courtesy, prudence and initiative, as a start.

Adaptability was of prime importance because the secretary had to work harmoniously with her boss, even if he were unbearable and she had to find a way to relegate her own feelings to the background and be loyal to him. She also had to be prepared to adapt herself to a completely different character when a successor took his place or when she changed her employment.

Resourcefulness was the quality most required when the boss was secretive, or forgetful, or a genius, or just dumb (some really were!) Then the secretary had to keep two jumps ahead of him and prevent him as diplomatically as possible from getting into hot water. Here the need for tact arises, how to correct his spelling and grammar so he thought he himself had written a fine letter or how to tell him he would miss the deadline on a report if he didn't get down to it at once. Tact was especially important in dealing with people who wanted to see or speak to him, especially if he didn't want to see or speak to them. The situation might call for a categoric 'no', a gentle 'no', a suggestion to write and make an appointment, or other evasive tactics which would not reflect badly on the Company as a whole or the boss in particular.

Serenity was also important. Many things can go wrong or occur all together and it is easy to become flustered or agitated when there is a simultaneous spate of telephone calls, claims for information, a search for somebody who seems to have gone to ground, and the alarm sounding for a fire practice. It may not be in one's character to remain cool in emergencies but a good secretary had to discover the way to train herself to acquire this virtue. It was indispensable.

As in other walks of life, courteous treatment can be repaid a hundredfold. Courtesy disarms resentments and annoyances and ensures co-operation and reciprocation. As the tendency today is always dynamic action, courtesy has suffered greatly. It is worth making every effort to bring it back even at this late stage.

Prudence covered many useful aspects of a secretarial position. Private or confidential matters never had to transcend through the medium of the secretary. She would never discuss such subjects with friends or relatives, in fact, she had to remember that the word secretary derives from 'secret'. Her responsibilities were not only to write letters and answer the telephone but to be the custodian of the confidential matters which were part of her job.

Initiative was often a very desirable attribute in the secretary but there are people who do not appreciate this, especially men newly promoted to responsible positions and nervous of their success. It therefore behoved the secretary to find out as quickly as possible how much of her own initiative she could safely use. Eventually, of course, as he settled down or came to depend on the abilities of his secretary, he would rely on her more and more, perhaps without realizing it.

One memorable boss who proved the necessity of most of the above qualifications was a prominent scientist who had been persuaded to join the Company to develop some 'indigenous technology'. He had put his talents at the disposal of industry with no few misgivings. It was a source of wonder to him that he could get up at six in the morning the four seasons of the year in order to be at the plant at eight. He marvelled even more that he had learned to hold his peace and submit to the outrageous stupidity of the Company bureaucrats who handled costs and audits and personnel matters. At first he had raged at them saying that his purpose in life was science and not filling in forms or counting the number of pencils used in the last six months.

Later he discovered that by paying lip service to them he could still go his own way and at the same time keep them out of his hair. But in spite of his efforts to the contrary he generated continual static and sometimes outright explosions which inevitably led to the final Big Bang over the incompatibility between this particular Man of Science and the Captains of Industry. The fact that I had found being his secretary very stimulating and enjoyable was regarded by Management as practically subversive. But the big corporation, because of its very nature, cannot tolerate the individualist, the maverick. The organization still needs the occasional brilliant talent but only as long as it conforms to the sacred principles of hierarchical management and demonstrates that the said talent will bring a Return on Investment.

At one time, for a few years I was secretary to the Chief Engineer in charge of construction and expansion of a leading plant in the Buenos Aires area. He was a New Zealander who had turned up in Argentina in the twenties for the building of the first subway in Buenos Aires city and he had an inexhaustible supply of yarns about his adventures around the world. His eagle eye for spotting defects and mistakes in the machinery and installations and his undiplomatic, forthright comments made him respected, but unpopular, among workers and supervision alike. He and his family became good friends of ours and when he retired and returned to New Zealand we kept up correspondence for many years. I think at first he found New Zealand a little too respectable and dull after Argentina. On one occasion when he was complaining about some New Zealand custom he was admonished: 'Look, Tommy, don't you start any Latin American antics here!'

I would also like to describe here one company where I worked for quite a long time, because it was by no means typical of local industrial complexes.

It was one of the much-maligned transnationals though, since a small percentage of the capital was Argentine-owned, the firm was obviously more tolerable and this native portion of capital was very useful in times of strident nationalism that governments now and then resorted to for rallying the boys around the flag. If the multinational corporations in general constitute some sort of threat to mankind, this one had many saving graces which made it an outstanding model for local industry, not that local industry showed much interest in emulating it.

The objective of private activity and business is primarily to obtain a return on the investment but this corporation, a chemical company, considered that equally important as profit, or even more so, was safety. Not surprisingly this philosophy originated in its earliest days in the U.S. when its first product was gunpowder. Constantly updated and improved, the safety manuals covered every process step, every construction large or small, every installation, every operation, right from the handling of nitroglycerine to closing the filing cabinet drawers without nipping one's fingers. The whole area of the plant with its five different factories was covered by a complete fire-fighting strategy, there were special provisions for disasters of different magnitudes and constant fire drills and training practices were part of life.

The basic step in this preparedness was a high degree of scrupulous cleanliness and order. A scrap of paper on the ground, a trickle of oil from a machine, a rusty nail, all deserved severe reprimands. The whole complex was continually patrolled by supervisors and foremen, while the top manager himself rarely missed his daily trip round the plants. New personnel often found all this incomprehensible but on the whole they soon became converted and began to spread the safety-first 'gospel' in their homes and among friends.

Plant operators and employees were very proud of the safety records constantly being won and surpassed. It was also a source of pride to work in conditions of safety and cleanliness when carelessness and unconcern over hazards characterized industrial concerns. Groups of operating personnel who were taken on visits to factories where their own production was being processed into end products, were shocked at the disregard for safety evident on all sides.

The singular, unflagging obsession of the firm with its safety objectives was not, of course, due to a humanitarian, benevolent Board of Directors ready to sacrifice profits for its employees' wellbeing. Prosaically, but not cynically, their argument was that people work better in humane, safe, clean conditions and when they are aware that their life and integrity have first priority. Then, in addition, the immense costs of insuring a huge chemical plant, with its multiple inherent risks, become significantly lower and the same is true for additional expenditures due to lost man-hours, accidents, indemnities and the various minor and major disasters occurring daily throughout industry.

The company had its own energy and water systems to cover all its needs. At the time I worked there, power cuts and water shortages were chronic in the Greater Buenos Aires district, so it became almost customary for the company to help make up the local town's deficits at critical hours. The water treatment system, also, was exemplary and the River Plate itself probably received no purer used water in all its course.

This example of what might be termed 'enlightened management' naturally extended into the field of labour problems and employee benefits. It seemed to me at the time that the firm was way out front in personnel relations and certainly it was a pioneer in Argentina where concern for the workers was claimed to be the exclusive province of the trade unions. Perhaps some unions cared for their affiliates but the large, powerful ones had other things in mind. The delegates in the company were regularly hauled over the coals by their union bosses because there were rarely any labour problems in the factory that could be convincingly inflated into a pretence for strikes. The operators as a whole showed no interest and if there were no real conflicts, the message from the bosses was . . . 'well, provoke some! Or else . . .'

Looking back now, far removed in time and place, on those years of Argentine hopes and disappointments in development, *coups d'état*, trade union agitation and guerrillas, climaxing in the disastrous military process which started in 1976, I can regard my time with the company as a valuable, enriching experience. Herewith my recognition: Ducilo S.A. (DUPONT DE NEMOURS)

Secretarial work has been largely a woman's occupation. Nowadays many other types of work are open to women so perhaps the demise of the secretary will pass more or less painlessly. Nevertheless, there is another very important problem of women's work which clamours for a solution.

The need to go out to work affects many women and is the subject of continual study by sociologists, philosophers, politicians and varied specialists. To speak from my own experience, it is a painful decision to have to leave the children in someone else's care and give full attention and energy to a job in order to help make ends meet. It is high time to recognize that the care and rearing of children is the most important task in all the world.

By now it is clearly apparent everywhere that some of the most excruciating problems of modern times can be traced back to the mistaken attitudes towards a child's early years.

The presence of the mother in the home is essential for the youngest children and advisable for the older ones. If the future adults, the most important resources of any country, are to be mentally and physically sound, the child-rearing tasks are the foundation for all other activities.

Industries and trade would be unable to thrive or even function if the people employed in them did not have someone at home to take care of the children, to train and teach them, to clean, to wash, to iron, to shop, to cook, to sew, to garden, to balance the family budget, in other words, to do the housework. The economics of business, however, does not take this into account. It is as if there were a vast body of slave labour, if we understand 'slave' as 'unpaid'. Yet all those tasks mentioned above have a monetary value, as anyone can prove by trying to hire the services of a nursemaid, a housemaid, a washerwoman, a cook, a dressmaker, a gardener and a chauffeur.

Why is it considered impossible, impracticable, delirious or even degrading to pay the housewife for the incomparable responsibility of her work? The mechanics of such a scheme can be demonstrated to be perfectly feasible. It is the philosophy of the idea which must be made convincing.

How many women would prefer to go out to work if they had a small income of their own which would help them feed, clothe and educate the children? Before the feminists shoot me down in flames, they should remember that a woman who is a mother and a housewife, yet in addition to that has to travel to work, meet the demands of her job, and still be a happy human being, will find small comfort in aggressive claims about women's rights. Why should it be a woman's right to work for nothing?

Physiologically and psychologically, a woman is a home-maker, her instincts are motherly, and her situation only becomes deteriorated by piling upon her more and more burdens. It is argued that by staying at home she cannot develop her potentialities as a human being, she is cut off from interaction and communication with the big world outside. Surely that is a vain postulation. A woman with a double load of home and job has precious little time or energy left to acquire any additional accomplishments or, even at the lowest level, to keep awake watching television.

The remuneration paid to housewives would go back almost at once into circulation, increasing purchases of food, clothing and household articles, thus benefitting wide sectors of trade and industry. With money available to buy better food and clothes, the children's health would inevitably improve.

There would be more jobs available for men if many women could withdraw from the labour market. From all we read in the newspapers and hear from politicians and bureaucrats, unemployment is a most serious problem in many parts of the world.

Here in Argentina serious work was done in the Fundación Bariloche, headed by Dr. Carlos Mallmann, on devising the mechanics of remunerating housework and child-rearing, as well as research into the participation of women in the processes of modern life. This is by no means a recommendation that women should not have a career or time-occupying outside activities, or that we should return to the old *Kinder, Küche und Kirche* model. Nevertheless, child-rearing and home-making deserve first priority and bold, imaginative measures should be put into practice to help women dedicate themselves wholeheartedly to their family if they so choose.

As regards women's liberation, it is obviously nonsense to claim physical equality, though we are all familiar with the enthusiasm men show about the equal right to stand in the crowded train or bus. In some countries women found they had the right to be street-sweepers, mechanics and bricklayers. Perhaps some women enjoy these occupations but I suspect they are the exception.

A woman may be a skilful driver but when her car gets a flat tyre she is unlikely, as well as unwilling, to change the wheel all by herself. Broadly speaking the most that can be expected of a woman in the maintenance of a car is to lift the bonnet from time to time and maybe pour in the required amount of oil. Even if she wants to understand how a machine works, a woman seems to be constitutionally unable to visualize the mechanisms in action, much less to become enthusiastic over them. Many housewives have learned of necessity how to fix a fuse or unstop a choked bathroom pipe, but they don't enjoy these jobs, supposedly any more than a man enjoys darning his socks.

Legally and theoretically women were for centuries, and still are in many places, in an inferior situation to men but nevertheless in practice it has been suggested in doubtful clichés that, for instance, the hand that rocks the cradle rules the world and one should never underestimate the power of a woman.

Now what is that power and how should it be used? Here it would seem that it is the women who have let the side down. They rocked the cradle but they did not teach their sons that women had equal rights as human beings, that they deserved real respect or that the division of tasks between men and women stems from the different physical and physiological aptitudes and not from superior or inferior endowments. They taught their daughters to be content with running a household, finding a husband who would take care of them and how to sew or paint pretty pictures rather than study mathematics or Latin or history and be scoffed at as a blue stocking.

Did the famous queens in history ever appoint women as Ministers or Secretaries of State? Did they do anything at all to improve the situation of their sisters? Queen Elizabeth I of England, playing to a male gallery, in fact the troops at Tilbury, announced, 'I know I have the body of a weak and feeble woman but I have the heart and stomach of a king . . .' She certainly acted in the masculine tradition when she felt her position threatened by the presence of another woman, Mary Queen of Scots, by having her decapitated, just in case.

So what was the power of a woman that was not to be underestimated? Tinkering behind the scenes, boudoir intrigues, calculating coyness?

The future certainly looks more hopeful for women in what is considered the sphere of Western civilization or influence and all those who have entered wholeheartedly into the struggle for recognition deserve women's gratitude, even if there are differences of opinion over particular methods, or scope or objectives. Much greater effort and energy will be required to alleviate the conditions of women in some other cultures where degradation and downright cruelty are their daily fare. The unjust, irritating discriminations against women which have aroused Western consciousness (and some consciences) are trivial in comparison.

The movements of women's liberation, however, will backfire on the very women they seek to liberate if they persist in aggressive, masculine tactics and attitudes. If it is the general opinion that men have made a mess of managing world affairs since the beginning of human history, it would be the utmost folly for women to continue along similar lines. It would appear that both virtues and vices tend to be more pronounced in women than in men. As Kipling remarked, the female of the species is more deadly than the male and he could have added that conversely, she can rise to greater heights, although perhaps he did not think so. When Eve induced Adam to disobey the one condition imposed on them by God in the earthly Paradise, she gave the excuse to all succeeding men for relegating women to an inferior category.

Adam's petulant reply to God, blaming 'The woman you gave me' for having led him into sin, is one clue to man-woman antagonism. The male imagery and patriarchal attitude which has come to dominate Western religious language is well described in *Words and Women* by Casey Miller and Kate Swift. The original Hebrew *adham* was translated into English as 'man' when it really was a generic term for 'humankind'. Further, 'the female imagery of God which is clearly present in the Hebrew Scriptures along with male imagery has often been ignored in English translations'. In developing their interesting chapter on The Language of Religion, from which the above quotations have been taken, the authors do not, however, examine the Catholic attitude to the Woman whose consent and participation in the redemption of human-kind was essential.

If the blame for the Fall must be placed upon Eve, then the merit for redressing the situation belongs to another woman, Mary the Mother of Jesus. What an immense tragedy that for nearly all Christians except Catholics Our Lady is relegated to a position of unimportance in the human relationship with God. Here is a woman placed above all other creatures, including the angels. What greater instrument of women's liberation could there be? When the Reformers removed her from her central rôle as the Mother of God, the fate of women in general became increasingly adverse, culminating in the situation which has in this century provoked feminist reaction against male tyranny.

Interest in religion seems to have become respectable in the lofty regions of academic research and thought where, up to the 1960s, it had belonged to the category of myth and where God was confidently considered to be dead. Yet by the end of the next decade and at the beginning of the 1980s the social scientists who had been studying the development processes taking place throughout the world were admitting that the human being requires some form of religion, that material progress or development had been little short of disastrous without a spiritual or non-material accompaniment. Maybe the overthrow of the Shah of Iran and the return to what was regarded as an impossibly medieval, anachronic regression, drove home to social scientists and development researchers the strength of religious sentiments and the grave dangers inherent in ignoring them. It is also probable that the charismatic figure of John Paul II at the same time has made an indelible impression on the minds of scientists and intellectuals who previously considered the subject of religion unworthy of their attention. It is interesting how often the name of Pierre Chardin de Teilhard appears in both learned and popular style articles and papers. Perhaps he was the prophet sent to heal the breach between science and religion.

Religious practices which had been thrown overboard at the time of the Protestant Reformation have been reappearing in somewhat different guise. Interest in mysticism and the habits of meditation are back again and respectable, thanks to the curiosity about Oriental religions and philosophies which swept Western civilization during the last decades. They have been shown to be an invaluable therapy for the stress-driven, harassed inhabitant of the aggressive environment in which millions of Western citizens attempt to achieve the material success demanded of them.

Even the physicists have had to admit that physics is no longer the coldly precise mathematical subject it was once considered to be. Quantum mechanics, quasars and black holes have changed all that precision. The physicist-philosopher Fritjof Capra in his celebrated *Tao of Physics* writes of how the 'dance' of the atoms in Buddhist concepts coincides amazingly with the discoveries of particle physics. Perhaps the despised Medieval theologians who speculated so uselessly – according to more enlightened beings – on how many angels could dance on the head of a pin, were in fact glimpsing the same vision.

The sacrament of Confession, now known as Reconciliation, was also the favourite target of the severest criticism. Yet nothing could be more up to date and chic than lying on the psychiatrist's couch and pouring out the sordid, miserable details of the one's life to a professional who may or may not have the right answers. He will certainly charge a fat fee for listening. The truth is that the human being sooner or later must unburden himself of his problems for the sake of his mental and psychological health so that the arguments in favour of such spiritual 'spring-cleaning' are founded on solid, human grounds, quite apart from the religious aspects.

Thomas Merton provides another example of the renewed interest in philosophical and religious subjects, his first book, *The Seven-Storey Mountain*, reaching best-seller status and his subsequent publications being eagerly awaited for their powerful message. Graham Greene, Morris West and Evelyn Waugh come to mind as novelists who have competently incorporated provocative, stirring religious themes into novels, whereas the books of Rabbi Chaim Potok are almost beyond description in the strength and poignancy of the religious themes they develop with such intensity.

No, God is not dead and religion is not the opium of the people. Human beings have invoked the name of God in vain and have used religion to justify innumerable crimes and cruelties but that does not abolish God or invalidate religions. To quote J.C. Squire:

God heard the embattled nations sing and shout
'Gott strafe England!' and 'God save the King!'
God this, God that, and God the other thing -
'Good God', said God, 'I've got my work cut out!'

The growing conviction throughout the world that material progress is not enough, should be a source of consolation to the hard-pressed modern human being. It is to be hoped that this conviction will be taken up by the young generations now forming and that they will turn to spiritual development as a first priority.

Not long ago I read a paper on behavioural problems and proper human development by a social science researcher, unconnected with any religious movement or confession. She presented it as an original contribution at an international gathering and it was decidedly well written. But, original? It was as if she had just stumbled on the Sermon on the Mount or the Theological Virtues. Her thesis was that the human being can only reach full physical and mental development through a series of attitudes and practices expressed in social science terminology but which boiled down to the homely tenets of simple faith.

I suspect that one of the reasons for my curiosity about the Roman Catholic Church was the insistence by Protestants in general and Presbyterians in particular that it was the root of most of the world's troubles. The poor in Ireland, for instance, were poor because they had to surrender to the Church the little money they had. It was the Church of the poor, the maids, labourers, dockers and crooks.

The Scots Presbyterian churches were obsessed with their anti-catholicism. To kneel in prayer, to wear a crucifix, to indulge in religious activity on any day except Sunday were Papist practices. In Scotland, repugnance for anything Catholic was so pronounced that Christmas Day was a working day and festivities were restricted to the pagan New Year's Day or Yuletide. Yet Good Friday in my hometown in north-east England and perhaps in others, was a holiday. The schoolchildren marched around the town square and each child received an orange from the Mayor! What the theological basis was for that ritual I cannot imagine now.

Nevertheless, there was a subconscious recognition of certain

Catholic attitudes which now and then unwittingly surfaced. Once when our Sunday School children were behaving in unruly fashion inside the church, the superintendent remonstrated sharply with them and made the extraordinary (to me) statement: 'If this were a Catholic church there would be none of this behaviour. Catholics are reverent and respectful in God's House.' That was enough to stir my curiosity about the fascinating enigma of whether Catholics were Christians or anti-Christians.

Another incident occurred when a local Catholic became the Mayor of our town. The Mayor's period of office, which lasted one year, was always inaugurated with a religious service in his respective church, and attended by all the Councillors and other members of the Mayor's Office. The fact that these worthy citizens would have to attend a Catholic Mass was presumably for some a shattering experience.

There was real indignation among the Presbyterians that one of their flock, many years a lady councillor, had the nerve to join the Mayor's party at the service. Perhaps she felt so strongly confident of her own views that nothing bad could happen to her by being courteous enough to respect the Mayor's convictions. She went so far as to write a note on the ceremony in the local newspaper and referred to the appropriate solemnity of the occasion and remarked on the reverent behaviour of even a humble message-boy, kneeling with the congregation. Judging by the comments, which naturally piqued my curiosity more than ever, the lady councillor had been most unwise both in attending and in writing her article.

I was also very intrigued by the four or five children at school who were excused the morning prayer assembly because they were Catholics. They seemed normal enough but we wondered if they had a terrible life, harassed by the priests, and having to pay money all the time to their church. There was also a Jewish girl at the school at one time, who was left very much to herself, because Jews were completely alien and quite beyond comprehension which in retrospect seems strange in view of the Protestant passion for the Old Testament and their great familiarity with the biblical scene.

A more forceful contact with the Catholic world took place when a close school companion fell ill with a near-fatal peritonitis. Before

Work and Worship

World War II a simple appendicitis meant a serious operation and four weeks in hospital, while complications were dangerous and required the utmost care and skilled nursing so peritonitis was always desperate.

After my friend's operation, her Protestant doctor recommended interning her in a convent nursing home in Newcastle-on-Tyne because he said that only the finest attention would bring her through and that kind of attention could only be received in the convent. The reaction at home to this staggering situation was: 'Fancy waking up and finding a nun beside you! I think I would pass out altogether!' 'What must it be costing! A fortune!' In spite of this awful thought, I was allowed to go and see her several times, indeed it could hardly have been denied.

The only explanation of why nuns make better nurses than other women was that since they dedicate their whole lives to their vocation, they are not thinking about worldly affairs like dates, clothes and parties or trying to ensnare one of the doctors as a husband. So evidently some nuns were not as sinister as had been my impression. By the time I was 16 or 17 my curiosity about Roman Catholicism was insatiable and I very daringly entered a Catholic bookshop and came away with two or three pamphlets which I hoped would explain a few questions.

I read them fascinated but it was a problem to know where to keep them. The possibility that they might be found in my room at home was too awful to contemplate. They were never discovered so I must have hidden them well. With the outbreak of war and subsequent work away from home, interest in the topic subsided and, in fact, whenever it began to stir again, I pushed it away as too complicated. Finally, however, the circumstances forced me to look the problem squarely in the face and eventually to make a personal decision.

In Argentina religion suffered from a kind of schizophrenia as a result of the generalized local tendency to identify it with Right or Left, presumably due to the intensity of political polarization.

The great currents of colonization from Europe in the early years of this century brought with them strong anti-clerical sentiments which contributed to the activities of secret societies, direct official harassment, and a decay in religious observance. Subsequent renewed interest in religion tended, unfortunately, to be accompanied by 'sponsoring' from political movements, a process which could only be regarded as unhealthy and which led very broadly to a division into anti-communist Right and Theology-of-Liberation Left. The military dictatorship from 1976-1983 only exacerbated the situation and showed no reluctance to justify the bloody repression process as being in defence of Western, Christian civilization.

So maybe what Argentina needs is some home-grown saints. There are several very particularly Argentine candidates to sainthood said to be advancing along the canonization procedures.

Perhaps the most revered and invoked is Ceferino Namuncurá, son of a great Indian chief, mentioned later in the chapter on Patagonia. His mother was a white captive, Rosario Burgos, one of the hundreds of women carried away in the Indian raids during the long struggle against the invader.

He was born on 26 August 1885, on the feast day of St. Ceferino, hence his given name. His birth took place in the settlement known as Chimpay or 'resting place' in Mapuche language, awarded to the tribe by General Roca after the defeat of the Indians. Very little is known of his early infancy and in 1891 the family moved to other land assigned to them in the foothills of the Andes. In that wild, lonely region there was no school or church, so his life was spent in riding the countryside with companions of his own age, becoming an expert horseman and skilled in gaucho tasks.

He was very attached to his home life and he became aware of the poverty of the tribe as a whole, compared with the relative well-being of his own immediate family. When he was 11 years old, he made a great decision: he told his father he wanted to go to Buenos Aires to study so he could be useful to his defeated race.

Father and son set out on the long journey to Buenos Aires and after interviews at high level, Ceferino was located in one of the Navy's mechanical shops, a totally unsuitable assignment which caused him increasing distress. After a few months he was transferred to the Salesian Pius IX College in Buenos Aires where he began an extraordinary period of dedication to study.

Work and Worship

One of the College priests declared:

'If I were unaware of Divine intervention, I would not be able to explain this constant dominion over himself in a boy who, until he was 11 years old, knew practically nothing about religion and the means of grace. It is true that I admire the sanctity of a Dominic Savio, born into a Christian family and molded by a saint like Don Bosco. But even more I admire the virtue of a little Indian of the Pampa, born into a family not exactly formal and exposed to the bad examples of a defeated tribe which has unreservedly embraced the worse aspects of civilization.'

As his vocation developed in intensity, he kept always before him the objective of studying for the priesthood and his ardent desire to serve his people. His health, however, continued to decline and he was unable to move on with other young candidates to the priesthood. In 1902 he had left Buenos Aires in order to return to his native climate and to continue his studies in the imposing San Francisco de Sales College in Viedma, this city being the capital of what is now the Province of Rio Negro. He wrote many letters which have been preserved and they reveal a remarkable ability to write fluidly and simply, expressing his sentiments with uncommon grace, in a language which was certainly not his own.

In 1904 the Director of the Salesians in Argentina, Bishop Cagliero, was appointed Archbishop of Savaste in Italy and he decided to take Ceferino with him, in the hope that his health might benefit and allow him to continue studies to become a priest. In fact, the long sea voyage did bring about a notable improvement and he reached Turin full of hope. Mgr Cagliero presented him to Pope Pius X, to whom Ceferino poured out his heart, telling of his yearning to become a priest and entreating him on behalf of his faraway brethren. The tuberculosis was, unfortunately, by now beyond cure and he gradually realized that his end was near. His hopes, illusions, dreams of converting his poor Mapuche tribe so far away in Argentina, faded one by one and he knew he would never return there. On 11 May 1905, as the dawn broke upon the Roman countryside, he expired, at the age of 19. When Pius X heard of his death he exclaimed: 'He was a beautiful hope for the Patagonian missions but from now on he will be their most valuable protector.'

To the Salesians he is: 'a flower plucked from the desert thornbushes, a rare precious lily of the Patagonian pampa, worthy to be held up as an example to civilized youth'.

In 1972, Pope Paul VI declared him Venerable and it is hoped that he will soon be canonized.

Another Patagonian candidate for sainthood is Italian-born Artémides Zatti, known as the Enfermero Santo de la Patagonia. He was born in Boretto, Reggio Emilia, in 1880 and came with his parents and six brothers and sisters to Argentina in 1897 when conditions in Italy were extremely difficult for the poor and Argentina was the destination of large currents of Italian immigrants. Unable to study for the priesthood due to poor health, he became a pharmacist and in 1906, as a Salesian lay brother, joined the San José Hospital run by the Order in Viedma.

The pharmacy of the hospital gave free assistance and medicine to the needy and in 1911, when the director of the hospital, Father Garrone, died, Zatti took upon his shoulders the administration of the entire hospital.

His whole life was a strenuous, unselfish dedication to the sick and poverty-stricken, depending almost entirely on faith in Divine Providence to supply the daily needs of the hospital which, like the pharmacy, was free for those without resources. Many stories are told of Don Zatti, as he was called affectionately by the population, of his daily rounds on his bicycle to visit patients, of his struggles to pay the bills for supplies, of his five days in jail on a trumped-up charge, of his innumerable kindnesses and complete dedication to the suffering, all this at a time when public social services barely existed in Argentina and were non-existent in most of the provinces.

In August 1950 he was found to be suffering from cancer of the pancreas. He continued to work while he could get about, and made jokes about the increasing yellow colour of his skin as the illness advanced. 'I'm ripening,' he explained, 'like a melon.' In March 1951 he died, amid the most profound consternation of all around him. The whole city closed down on the day of his funeral and since then the cause for his beatification has progressed firmly.

In the Province of Córdoba, the venerable figure of the Cura Brochero, stands out among many famous sons and daughters of the region. The province is situated approximately in the geographical centre of the country and is a favourite vacation land, with its benign climate and fine scenery of hills and mountains. The eastern part of the province marks the end of the broad pampa and the beginning of the sierras or ridges which, further westwards, swell to the Andean foothills. It has a rich colonial heritage and the capital, Córdoba City, boasts a 400-year history as a centre of learning and erudition, with its university founded in 1613. Since the middle of this century, however, it has also developed into a great industrial area, particularly automobile and aircraft construction.

The inhabitants of the province possess a very strong local sentiment, along with a highly distinctive inflection of speech. They are descended from industrious pioneers who, with simplicity and tenacity, sprinkled the fertile valleys with fruit farms and small, unpretentious towns that are now the delight of visitors from congested, over-urbanized areas.

In the western part of the province where the mountain range is more rugged and imposing, its highest peak being the Campaquí, 9,000 feet above sea level, one of these small towns is known as Villa Cura Brochero. Until 1916 it was called Villa El Tránsito but the name was changed to honour the legendary priest, José Gabriel Brochero, who laboured there long and lovingly.

He was born in 1840 in the hill town of Santa Rosa. His parents were poor by material standards but through years of honest, hard work and modest ambitions, they were able to make fair progress. José Gabriel sang his first Mass in 1866, at a particularly dark period of Argentine history.

There had been political upheavals and dissensions, and in 1877 cholera broke out in Buenos Aires and spread to Rosario and Córdoba. Father Brochero, with other priests and friars worked incessantly taking assistance to the sick and dying. Anecdotes and legends about him are innumerable, for he had an unusual manner and a forthrightness in all his actions. He identified himself completely with his humble parishioners, dissimulating his own innate culture under an outward appearance of the utmost simplicity, so that he could reach their hearts more effectively.

Ahead of his time in his pastoral and missionary ideas, Father Brochero was indefatigable in efforts to serve, evangelize, educate, encourage, exhort and seek better conditions of life for his hard-pressed flock. He rode continually over his rugged parish, a familiar figure on his famed sturdy horse, out at whatever time of day or night and in whatever weather, under the scorching summer sun or in the wild storms of winter. At some time in these labours he contracted the dread disease of leprosy and his life ended with blindness, pain and physical collapse, in a dramatic immolation of self for the love of Our Lord.

Almost contemporary with Father Brochero, Franciscan Friar Mamerto Esquiú (pronounced Es-kee-you), whose cause for beatification is said to be well-advanced, is renowned for his oratory, especially his sermon in 1852 on the proposed Argentine Constitution. He was born in 1826 only ten years after Argentina's Independence, into a humble farm family in the northern Province of Catamarca. It is a majestic land near the Tropic of Capricorn, where the Andean peaks rise to over 18,000 feet. His early years were lived during a period of internal struggle which threatened to tear the new country apart.

The protracted anarchy, despotism and instability finally came to an end in 1852 and a Constitution, inspired in the U.S. model, was drawn up. An important fraction of the population, however, opposed it strongly and it was at that time Fray Mamerto delivered his great sermon, urging the adoption of the Constitution which would bring peace to the strife-ridden nation. The magnificent text of his sermon has been preserved and though perhaps too florid and declamatory in style for modern taste, it is easy to see how its impact contributed so strikingly to the overwhelming acceptance of the Constitution.

Nevertheless, his great success as an orator was precisely the cause of his deepest spiritual suffering. Everywhere he went he was praised and applauded but in reality he sought the silence and humility of his real vocation and in 1862 he departed for a Franciscan convent in Tarija, Bolivia. When in that country he founded a newspaper in which he strenuously promoted adherence to the Pope, then under

Work and Worship

military attack by Garibaldi and the King of Italy, Victor Manuelle.

In 1872 he was dismayed to learn that the Argentine government had nominated him Archbishop of Buenos Aires but he was able to have the decision annulled. Eight years later, however, he was unable to refuse the designation as Bishop of Córdoba made directly by Pope Leo XIII, although he did continue to wear his coarse Franciscan habit at all times. After two strenuous years as bishop, he was suddenly taken ill in a remote part while on a long journey visiting his flock. He died a day or two later, on 10 January 1883.

Finally, it would be appropriate to mention the Patroness of Argentina, Uruguay and Paraguay, Our Lady of Luján.

Luján is the name of a city and a river about fifty miles west of Buenos Aires. The river, which seems to have received that name in 1541, winds slowly across the broad plains and eventually joins the great delta of the Paraná. The beginnings of the town, however, have been traced to 1682 when a portion of land was set aside for the construction of a chapel.

This land marked the site of a curious incident which had occurred back in 1630. Overland trade at that time was carried out in convoys of large wagons drawn by slow-moving teams of oxen and the route from Buenos Aires to Perú and the northern territories passed close to the river Luján where the drovers camped overnight. On this particular occasion one of the wagons in the convoy could not be moved the next morning when the journey was being resumed. The men removed most of the heavy cargo but still the wagon remained stuck. Finally, they took out two small boxes and the wagon moved forward.

The cargo was put back but whenever one of the boxes was loaded on to the wagon, no progress could be made. Intrigued, the wagoners opened it and found it contained a statue of Our Lady. They concluded that this was a sign from heaven that the statue was to remain there and so a simple oratory was hastily constructed to house it. The wagon train moved on and one of the few local settlers took care of the chapel until the time came to build a more lasting adequate home for Our Lady of Luján. The present basilica dates from 1873 and is the centre of pilgrimages from many parts of Argentina and South America.

This is surely a curious 'miracle', devoid of the dramatic events associated with other Marian sanctuaries. Here we have a group of humble drovers who, like the shepherds of Bethlehem, immediately understood the message and spread the news. In the words of the Argentine Episcopal Conference of 1980:

> 'In the year 1630 two simple statues of the Virgin Mary reached Luján on their way to Sumampa (Perú). The Virgin herself chose one of them to stay by the River Luján, and from there to lavish innumerable graces on Argentines and their brethren in neighboring countries.'

4

Flora and Fauna, among other things

Like many thousands of immigrants who, over the years, came to Argentina I settled down without difficulty. Moments of homesickness are inevitable, of course, and the cure would seem to be to pay a visit to the Old Country. A long absence from the familiar faces and scenes provokes a growing yearning and anxiety to return, no matter how satisfactory the situation may be in the place of exile.

The cure is usually rapid and enduring. Not all the old faces and scenes will still be there back home and the joy of seeing those who have remained is soon replaced by the realization that there have been too many changes. Fields and byways have vanished under asphalt and concrete, buildings have been razed and others have appeared. Friends and acquaintances are widely scattered, they have established new families and circles of friends, some have died, others have changed with maturity and are conditioned by the particular situations and circumstances which the exile has not shared. A few months or, indeed, a few weeks are enough to make him realize that the homesickness was illusory and he hurries back to mend his faraway fences, to focus his energies and affections on the present and the future.

New inhabitants of this country are often unaware that Argentina has cast a spell on them. It was common to hear Europeans grumbling about the inefficiency of public services, the unreliability of trains and buses, the disrepair of roads and sidewalks and a hundred other shortcomings which contrasted unfavourably with Europe. How many hundreds decided to go back after a few years, only to reappear in Argentina, perhaps less than a year after departing 'fed-up' and disappointed? It could be that Europe produced in them a sense of asphyxiation and regimentation in comparison with the uncluttered horizons and individualist existence in Argentina. It could be that efficiency and order did not entirely compensate for the intangible advantages which had been overlooked in trying to re-establish older habits in a totally different scene.

Argentina has been a successful melting pot for people from many parts of the world and though immigration has dried to a mere trickle, she still receives foreigners without friction. It could also be the friendliness and affability of the Argentines themselves. Foreigners, from wherever they may come, are welcome on their individual merits. Income or lack of it will not automatically raise a barrier and the man who progresses in the world does not normally snub his friends of more modest times.

Doubtless the attitude towards family life is a great source of strength. It is true that the disruptive tendencies of the times are evident at all levels and particularly in the over-large cities. To become friendly with an Argentine family means becoming acquainted quickly with brothers- and sisters-in-law, uncles, aunts, grandparents and nephews to an extent that would surprise even Sir Joseph Porter, K.C.B. These families are not necessarily models of love and harmony and they have their share of squabbles and dramas but the bonds of blood and sentiment are strong when difficult circumstances assail the family.

The immigrant couple who settle in this country cannot help but compare the solitary struggle to progress with that of their neighbours surrounded by numerous relatives who can help each other in time of need. The day comes, of course, when the immigrants' children grow up and marry. With the first marriage not only a son- or daughter-in-law is acquired but, for better or worse, a host of new relations.

My own experience was that I married in Argentina without being able to make any 'sentimental journey home', so when the long-postponed trip took place, we had three small children and a fourth on the way. To bring up four children is no small matter, as anyone who has attempted it is well aware.

As occurs much too often, I had very little idea of what would be involved. Maybe, in the past, when families were very large and the elder children helped with younger ones and all had their special chores assigned to them, they came to marriage with a considerable amount of practical knowledge. In these days of training and specialization in all branches of knowledge and activities, when six or seven years at the university are required to become a doctor or an engineer or a lawyer and other professions may demand even more training and formation, no particular qualifications are required for the world's most complicated, transcendent task: to rear a family.

When I was aware of what lay in store for me, I bought a hefty American 'how-to' book, which explained in careful detail minute-by-minute, blow-by-blow instructions for a zero defects performance from the baby's birth to 1 year of age. Naturally, the defects on my part started from the very beginning and by the time the baby was 3 months old, I had abandoned most of the recommendations as impractical or impossible, at least as far as I was concerned. The first child, in spite of being something of a guinea-pig, managed to survive and she was followed by two brothers and a sister, this being considered by more prudent relatives and friends as absolute recklessness.

At the time of our trip to Europe, the normal way to travel was by sea and there were many fine comfortable transatlantic liners on the regular South American routes. Now in these days of air travel there are only a few cargo vessels with accommodation for perhaps a dozen passengers. Swept away into the past are the noisy scenes on the docks at the departure of these great ships carrying several hundred passengers. Our ship, the French liner *Louis Lumière* was headed for Mediterranean ports and finally Genoa, so the dock was crowded with a waving, cheering, singing throng of Italians, giving their relations an emotional send-off that was quite fascinating and unimaginable in an airport today.

After a few hours, when nearing Montevideo just across the River Plate, 18-months old Monica suddenly developed a raging fever. The ship's doctor immediately quarantined her and me in the isolation bay and we were there for four days until the attack disappeared as quickly as it had come. It had been a very worrying time, as she lay on the bed rigid as a china doll and it was only some days later that the doctor said he had suspected infantile paralysis, since there was an epidemic of polio in Argentina at the time.

This epidemic was the subject of bitter reproaches against the Peronist régime after the fall of Perón in 1955 because it had found the hospitals completely unprepared and without equipment such as iron lungs, in those days about the only effective measure for reducing some of the dreadful effects of the illness. Many imposing hospitals had been built but they lacked even the most elementary materials and were little more than empty shells. Furthermore, the authorities had clamped down on all information or comments by the media, so the ordinary citizen was unaware of the gravity of the situation and only heard alarming rumours or learned of specific cases from acquaintances.

It seems likely that Monica did really have polio but fortunately it was without consequences, apart from immunizing her effectively from further attacks.

The journey thereafter continued normally. The meals were very good, even in our tourist class where normally it was accepted that food would be modest and it seemed to us that the popular conception of French cuisine as being better than most was in fact confirmed. The long sea journey was a very special experience, even with the constant anxiety of ensuring that the children would not fall overboard. It was a total disconnection from the past and future for twenty days, a self-contained community of passengers with varied origins and conditions, with time to read and relax and enjoy conversation.

Today sea journeys appear to be mostly pleasure cruises with every possible sort of entertainment and guided activities for pampered vacationers and I imagine there are twenty-four hour connections by telephone and telex and satellites with the rest of the world.

About all the organized entertainment we had was the daily betting on the distance travelled and the ceremony of crossing the Equator. The ocean of the Tropics has a most beautiful, unique blue colour. Perhaps we can some day take another sea trip and marvel at the sea and the sky, the luminescence of the ship's wake, the occasional

Flora and Fauna, among other things

whale spouting in the distance, the leap of some great fish from the waves, the delightful spectacle of flying fish and dolphins racing ahead of the bow.

The ship called at Santos, where we bought some bags of coffee beans, since at that time coffee was very scarce in Europe. The beans later helped to enhance our welcome, though officials in the various Customs we passed through regarded them doubtfully, probably suspecting they would find their way to the black markets in scarce commodities still flourishing after the war. Rio de Janeiro and Bahia were other ports of call, both of them unforgettably fascinating and then, at the other side of the Atlantic, Dakar.

We had only one day there, but it was also highly memorable, particularly the Senegalese inhabitants, so tall, dignified and handsome and wearing robes of the most resplendent colours. Our eldest child, 4-year-old Mary, was astounded that the people had such black skins and the explanation that there was uncommonly strong sunshine in Dakar seemed to satisfy her, though she commented that the coal-black babies riding in the folds of the mother's ample robes had hardly had time to get so sunburned.

On preparing to leave Dakar, we watched hundreds of young Senegalese soldiers marching into the depths of the ship en route for Indo-China. It was impossible not to feel a heavy sadness over their probable fate far from their own land. I often remembered that day at Dakar when in subsequent years the terrible slaughter in places like Dien Bien Phu must have claimed the lives of many of those men.

Back in Europe, after the first effusions of reunion following long absence, it gradually became evident that re-adaptation was going to be difficult. In the meanwhile, another boy was born. Paradoxically, he lightened our load as in some mysterious way he conquered the hearts of many who regarded us as irresponsible. When he was making his entry on the scene in Scotland, my mother took over care of the other three children. Since she lived for another thirty years after that, she obviously recovered well from the experience. The children were quite familiar with English but during the few months in Scotland, our second child, Joe, acquired a marvellous Scots accent, as well as words like coo, hoose and aye, especially aye. My mother disapproved of this and figured the children should learn to speak more conventional English, but the conversation which practically put an end to her efforts took place at the tea-table and went something like this:

Mother: Joe, would you like some cake?
Joe: Aye.
Mother: Joe, don't say aye, say yes.
Joe: Me wants cake.
Mother: Joe, don't say me, say I.
Monica: Don't say I, say yes!

A few months after this episode, we were once again on the ocean 'rolling down to Rio' and beyond. We had left the Port of London on a typically grey, overcast day, few people had been on the dock to wave goodbye to the ancient Royal Mail steamship. We were nursing mixed emotions, some guilt at being glad to go back to Argentina, eager for sunshine and diaphanous skies, and though it may seem strange, the certainty that back there we would feel at home again.

The trip was on the whole unremarkable. An Argentine actor who had gone ashore in Vigo failed to appear when the ship departed but he hired a taxi to take him to Lisbon and in what he referred to as a desperate dash throughout the length of Portugal, he was in Lisbon first and came once more aboard amid cheers and jokes of all kinds.

Somewhere off the Brazilian coast, an unfortunate passenger had an attack of madness and had to be locked up until he could be handed over to the hospital authorities in Rio de Janeiro.

About the same time I myself nearly had another kind of attack. Among the passengers was an elegant Hindu lady, wearing saris and typical Indian jewellery. She was often in our conversation groups and one evening when I brought the newly-bathed children into the lounge to wait for dinner, Joe who was especially rosy and shining like an apple, informed the group he had just had a bath. He thereupon addressed the Hindu lady: 'You need a bath, too!'

Through the suffocating confusion of embarrassment, I heard her answer serenely and without offence, 'No, little Joe. My skin is always that colour, even when it's washed.'

Perhaps she smiled inwardly at my scarlet hue but there is no

Flora and Fauna, among other things

doubt she was a model of equanimity and patience.

Soon we were back again in Argentina, which we really knew only superficially but which was to become our second homeland, where we would raise those four children and where now, from the sidelines, we offer them our invaluable advice on how to raise their own children.

To the rest of the world at large, Argentina is synonymous with gauchos, tangos, beef and, maybe, Maradona, but it is also the great Paraná river system with its fertile delta and exuberant vegetation, reaching into the heart of the continent to meet Paraguay and Brazil at the amazing Falls of Iguazú.

It is the Andes mountains soaring to their highest point of 18,000 feet, the Aconcagua and nearby, the dramatic statue of Christ the Redeemer at the border with Chile. It is the lush vineyards and gardens of Mendoza in the foothills of the Andes, the uplands of Salta and Jujuy with strangely-coloured mountains and canyons and picturesque towns; the bright red earth, the brilliant green vegetation of Misiones Province. It is Córdoba with its lovely hills and luminous skies; the rich farm lands of Buenos Aires Province and the seemingly endless plains of the Pampas.

Proceeding southwards, it is Patagonia abundantly fruitful along the river valleys and unbelievably beautiful in the region of lakes, mountains, forests and spectacular glaciers, stretching away to Tierra del Fuego. Across the wild Straits of Magellan lies the Antarctic with its scientific and naval bases, welcoming a few intrepid tourists in the brief summer. Argentina claims as its territory the land to the South Pole between longitudes 24° and 75° W. There have been permanent Argentine stations in the Antarctic since 1904 and even some children have been born there to wives of servicemen stationed in the area.

The Province of Buenos Aires where I lived for many years, is a low-lying, fertile sweep of farmland bounded on the north by the delta of the Paraná, on the east by a semicircle of continuous sandy beaches along the South Atlantic, on the west by the pampa rising gradually to meet the Andes and on the south by the semi-arid steppes of Patagonia.

The city of Buenos Aires grew much too large in recent decades although it still has its particular fascination: large parks, theatres, cosmopolitan restaurants and avenues lined with tropical and sub-tropical trees, such as the jacarandá (*Jacaranda mimosifolia*) with its graceful form awash in sky-blue flowers before the leaves appear. For about two weeks in November when they are in full bloom, the city is transformed. Another sub-tropical tree widely used in the city is the very tall, elegantly arching tipa (*Tipuana tipu*). In summer it gives an abundance of small bright yellow flowers which fall in great showers to carpet the sidewalks and line the streets with golden gutters. It is impossible to overlook the palo borracho (*Chorisia speciosa*) whose flowers are reminiscent of large, frilly orchids but it is the swollen, bottle-like appearance of its spiky trunk which singles it out as a curiosity and gives it its local name of *borracho* meaning drunk.

I remember how, just a few weeks after arriving in Argentina, I took a long ride on a beautifully warm evening through the suburbs in an old open tram. On both sides of the streets there were many paraíso or Paradise trees, at that time in flower. Their fragrance which filled the air, left no doubt about why they were so named, but if they are still there, the fumes from present-day intense traffic will surely obliterate their perfume. The tram-cars were scrapped years ago in the name of progress, mistakenly, I think.

Buenos Aires city is ringed by an overgrown urban sprawl that has ensnared numerous towns and suburbs, some of which have their own special charm. These suburbs abound in colourful gardens and heavily tree-lined streets. Maybe it is because of the trees that it is still possible to breathe in the city, as the quantity of noxious gases from vehicles must reach deadly proportions.

Naturally, the 300 miles of Atlantic beaches of the Province of Buenos Aires are easily accessible for weekends and longer holidays by the ocean. The beaches are linked by a chain of seaside resorts, culminating in the outsize holiday city of Mar del Plata. For reasons best known to themselves, the over-crowded residents of Buenos Aires pour into Mar del Plata in the summer to enjoy an even more overcrowded vacation. The other resorts vary all the way down the scale from large and noisy to very small and quiet, thereby catering for all tastes.

One of these seaside towns is Villa Gesell. It was the prototype for

Flora and Fauna, among other things

coastal developments and owes its existence to the vision and tenacity of a German immigrant engineer, Carlos Gesell. When he first regarded these Atlantic shores some seventy years ago, he was preoccupied with the threat posed by the extensive dunes advancing over farm and grazing land. So in 1931 he bought a large area of inexpensive dunes, thus creating doubts about his sanity, and he set to work on the first part of his vision.

Using various techniques for fixing the sand and fighting ants and snails, Gesell was rewarded with a rolling landscape of fast-growing pine, eucalyptus and acacia woods, running parallel to the golden beaches. He enlisted the help of two German brothers by the name of Lömpel, Enrique being an architect and Jorge a constructor. Together they projected the second part of the vision: a township of red-roofed, white chalets and the various utilities and amenities required to complete an original seaside resort sheltering from the ocean winds and the hot summer sun among the woods that had conquered the dunes.

Villa Gesell is possibly the only town in Argentina which has not been spread-eagled on the chequerboard design applied throughout the country for town planning since Colonial times but rather, the streets and avenues follow the contours of the land, twisting and curving naturally. It is now one of the larger and noisier places of the Atlantic coast and is a favourite of the younger people.

This was the scene of our very first family vacation in Argentina less than a year after our return from Europe. Then it was small and very quiet, only recently off the drawing board, so to speak. The beach stretched north and south to the horizon, the waves were great fun, the sand was warm and there were ponies and sulkies for riding through the young forest rising over the dunes.

Other schemes for fixing the dunes with grass and forests were carried out along the coast in succeeding years and have given rise to the great activity of the area, especially in summer. Another feature of this coast is the beautiful stands of pampa grass, so popular as an ornamental plant in European parks and gardens. Acres of tall, graceful plumes rippling in the sunlight create a lovely spectacle. In reality, it is found widely across the country and is known as *cortadera* because of its fine, sharp-edged leaves, or more popularly as *cola de zorro*, meaning fox's tail. Presumably in the past it spread across the untamed pampas that are now vast fields for grain and cattle.

This brings to mind a page of my primary school geography book in the chapter on a faraway country called Argentina, which for some reason I recall out of all the other forgotten subjects. There was an illustration showing the ears of a horse and the head of a gaucho visible above tall pampa grass and the text stated that it grows so high a man on horseback could ride through it unseen.

On these famous pampas or temperate zone grasslands, there is a curious native tree, the ombú (*Phytolacca dioica*), a massive squat plant which spreads out its branches over a radius of 180 feet, while its sprawling roots protruding from the ground like great tentacles, knot themselves into intricate patterns around the base of the trunk. George Pendle in his book, *Argentina* (1955), writes these interesting lines about the ombú:

Ombú

Flora and Fauna, among other things

'The ombú lives for innumerable years: no cyclone can blow it down, nor can fire destroy it; its pulpy wood is useless to man even as fuel. Thus, although it is a friendly tree for the rider and his mount when the sun is high, the ombú in reality is a lonely weed, a fit symbol of Argentina's solitude.'

To complete the picture, botanically speaking it is a variety of grass and not a tree at all.

The pampas or prairies of Argentina, which extend well beyond the Province of Buenos Aires, are the home of large numbers of birds. W.H. Hudson, the nineteenth-century naturalist born in this province, pioneered the study of Argentine birds and he is greatly revered in this country. He refers, for instance, to the chingolo, a small bird which accompanies human settlements '... wherever man constructs a house and plants a tree, the chingolo comes to keep him company.' It often suffers the imposition of the black tordo which, like the European cuckoo, lays its eggs in the nests of other birds. The female

Oven-bird and nest

chingolo incubates the eggs and raises the chicks, which are soon twice her size. According to Hudson the tordos '. . . since they have no domestic affairs of their own to attend to, live in flocks the whole year, leading an idle, vagabond life.'

One of the most popular birds north of Patagonia is the hornero or oven-bird. It has neither bright plumage, nor melodious song, nor brilliant flight, nor great size, which would give it renown. It is a light brown bird, the size of an English thrush and seems to seek human company. It constructs its mud nest, the size of a soccer ball, usually on the top of a fence post or on a ledge of a building. Urbanization, instead of driving it away, provides it with a suitable habitat. One of the most unexpected sites chosen some years ago by an oven-bird was the Independence Monument in the middle of the Plaza Mayo in the heart of Buenos Aires city. In the rural area it is considered a sign of good fortune and is an efficient guardian, giving noisy warning of potential danger.

At nest-making time the oven-bird secretes an abundant flow of saliva with which, using its beak as a bricklayer's trowel, it binds the mud with sticks, small roots, seeds, horsehair, straw and leaf scraps. Construction takes about six to eight days and the nest weighs finally about ten pounds. It has an oval entrance and a passage leading to two 'rooms', the parlour and the bedroom, the latter being lined with down and soft hay. The oven-bird pairs for life and in the countryside it is said that it scrupulously observes Sunday as a day of rest.

Sentinel of the prairie is the chajá, the size of a turkey, that paces the ground majestically and flies with eagle-like grace. However, the most striking feature of this bird is its nerve-wracking scream which effectively shatters the silence of the pampas.

Much smaller but equally vigilant is the tero, or plover. It is constantly on the alert and it is almost impossible to cross the open country without having a tero protesting overhead and, in the process, exciting all nearby teros into similar action. Tame teros are frequently seen in town gardens as a 'watchbird' instead of a watchdog. It is curious that in the little Andean town of El Bolsón, the teros seem to have adopted the place. They strut happily about their self-allotted territories among the grass and roses of the main avenue and in the gardens which they presumably consider suitable. Garden

Flora and Fauna, among other things

owners are said to feel flattered when a couple of teros adopt them and the birds' periodical shrill cries are regarded as a sort of early warning system, especially when the garden is large, as is frequently the case in these spacious regions.

Many small animals inhabit the Argentine pampas, a characteristic representative being the animal known elsewhere as the armadillo. It is the protagonist of a great number of legends and superstitions. Among the rural population there is a tendency to identify it with the weak, submissive personage that in the end defeats the big bully. It is omniverous, in fact its capacity is enormous. Probably its greatest originality is that all the embryos of each litter come from the same ovule, generating according to the species, between four and twelve identical offspring. In the seventies it was discovered that it could contract human leprosy, no other animal having been found which could be used for laboratory work in the search for a cure of the disease. To complete its versatility, its shell has been applied for many years as the sounding box of the charango, a musical instrument reminiscent of a small guitar.

Armadillo

Similarly identified with the rolling pampas is the vizcacha, famed for the extensive warrens it constructs, parts of which are sometimes taken over by other creatures, such as burrowing owls, rodents and even small snakes, while the whole area and its surroundings become thoroughly eroded of vegetation by the constant coming and going of the population. The vizcacha also collects twigs, dried thistles and stones and arranges them around the entrance to the warren. This has given rise to applying the name 'vizcacha' to a person who fills his house with all kinds of junk, while in other rural lore it appears as the personage who never pays his debts. One legend goes that the vizcacha used to buy his tobacco from the owl but when the owl came to demand payment, the vizcacha hid in his burrow. Since then, the owl is to be seen standing at the door of the warren waiting to collect his money.

Where the prairie lands reach the delta of the River Paraná, there is a remarkable change of scenery. This delta is only about twenty miles away from Buenos Aires city and is an intricate system of waterways and river branches, flowing among dense vegetation, citrus orchards and light timber plantations and, of course, it is an ideal place for all kinds of water sports. Above all, it is another lung to help the city to breathe.

This is where the vast river systems of northern Argentina, uniting to form the river Paraná or 'Father of the Waters' in Guaraní language, flow into the River Plate which, a mere sixty miles later, reaches the Atlantic. The systems are structured around three powerful rivers: the Uruguay, the Iguazú and the Paraná. The Uruguay joins the Paraná close to its junction with the Plate, while the Iguazú flows into it far to the north, a few miles downwaters of the Iguazú Falls on the frontier with Brazil. The Spanish explorers first saw these cataracts in 1542, consisting of more than 300 separate falls over a semicircle of basalt walls. The most impressive is the 200-foot Garganta del Diablo or Devil's Throat. Various walkways make it possible to reach exciting vantage points through the drenching spray which rises high above the falls and can be seen from a great distance across the tropical forest.

We visited Iguazú one year with my mother who had plucked up her courage and come to stay some months with us. First we had taken her 4,000 kilometres around Patagonia in the car. That had been quite an undertaking for her and it would not have been surprising if she had felt she had seen enough of Argentina for the time being. However, she had heard about the Falls and shortly before she returned to England we took her there by air so that the journey would be less strenuous for her.

The journey may have been less strenuous but it turned out to be more nerve-wracking. We ran into the full fury of a tropical storm which bounced the plane around through the blackest of black clouds amid violent lightning on all sides. At one time the plane shuddered as if it were a train with square wheels and when I looked anxiously and apologetically at my mother in this discomfort, she remarked cheerfully, 'It's a good thing I had so much practice riding all over Patagonia in your station wagon!'

The plane landed safely after giving the impression that it was about to nosedive into the wide river but the storm continued and seemed to follow us to the hotel. Just as the elevator reached our floor, the power for the whole town was cut off, in a deafening thunderclap. Fortunately we were able to open the door and step on to the landing.

The next day we went to a hotel much nearer the Falls, newly modern with air conditioning, so welcome in that steaming, tropical climate. However, the problem at that time, and presumably solved by now, was that if the hotel switched on its air conditioning, the power went off for miles around, so it was not used. There were only double rooms in the hotel and my mother wanted a single, arguing that it was a pity to pay for something you did not need. Since we stayed there two days, she solved the problem and made a further contribution to the family folklore by sleeping in one bed the first night and in the other the next. The spectacle of the Falls more than fulfilled our expectations and the short side trips to border towns in Brazil and Paraguay combined to put the visit to Iguazú in a landmark category.

It is interesting to reflect on the attraction of falling water, from little trickles streaming like lace over rocks and stones among ferns and hidden flowers, mountain streams leaping from one cascade to another, to the powerful impressive falls that become famous tourist centres. Even a modest, man-made weir adds a special beauty to any drab river. No wonder fountains in city parks and avenues are everywhere admired. I often wondered how I could find a way to get a little home-made waterfall in my flat Buenos Aires garden but the appropriate technology and the willing manpower never materialized though I did eventually have a lilypond with goldfish and tiddlers and water-lilies.

From Iguazú in the long journey to the sea the rivers are fed by innumerable tributaries, streams which tumble from the mountainous regions of the Mato Grosso of Brazil, others which meander slowly across the lowlands, creating vast swamps and strings of lagoons, often hidden below an exuberant carpet of floating vegetation. The region is liable to serious flooding as a result of the torrential rains of the tropics, covering millions of hectares with a sea of floodwater. The floating vegetation chokes the waterways and presses dangerously against bridges and other structures, while it carries as unwilling passengers many small and not-so-small creatures, including snakes and rodents, right to the South Atlantic. Among the floating plants are the prolific water hyacinths and the enormous irupé or water-lily whose leaves can measure two metres in diameter and whose edible seeds justify the popular name of water-maize.

This vast region, known as the Mesopotamia, is wonderfully fertile and produces many important crops like tea and rice and, of course, *yerba maté*, the national beverage. Argentines have converted this distinguishing feature of daily life into an idiosyncrasy. The *yerba* is brewed with very hot water in a gourd and then sipped through a *bombilla*, or small pipe, at any time, in any place. Even on the long-distance buses, the passengers often bring their equipment complete with thermos flask of hot water and serve themselves refreshing *matés* along the way.

The sub-tropical regions produce fine hardwoods, like palo santo (*Bulnesia sarmientoi*), with its dark green and brown graining, its fragrance and sacred connotations. Others have brilliant blossoms, for instance the lapacho (*Tabebuia ipe* and *T. avellanedae*) which flames along the Paraná river banks in an unforgettable springtime spectacle.

Perhaps the quebracho (from *quiebra-hacha* or axe-breaker) is the native Argentine tree best known outside the country. It takes 100 years to mature and relies on spontaneous generation for reproduction. There are two varieties, the colorado or red, and the blanco or white.

Quebracho wood is extremely hard and heavy, being almost indestructible under the severest conditions of weather and water. Its fame, however, derives from its exploitation for the extraction of tannin. Around 1850 a British company started these activities in the northern forests of Argentina and the tree became the symbol of the devastating colonial practices of foreign capital. When the quebracho came near to extinction, the company just moved out and headed for similar forests of tannin-producing trees in Africa. It left behind a trail of ghost towns, ravaged woodlands and unutterable bitterness.

The company had ruled its remote domain in the near-feudal fashion also known in North America, where the labourer is kept in permanent debt to the company by being forced to buy provisions from the Company Store at exorbitant prices. While this recalls the miners' song about digging Sixteen Tons, with its humorous overtones, the words and music of an Argentine song about the ghost town Villa Guillermina are plaintive and sad. Some years a local film called simply *Quebracho* was a vigorous, evocative indictment of this exploitation, but it was prohibited by the military dictatorship in case it offended the susceptibilities of International Capital.

An all-purpose tree *par excellence* is the versatile algarrobo (*Prosopsis ongra* and *P. alba*) which is a sub-tropical hardwood very widespread in the northern provinces. It is used for furniture, for building material, firewood, its seeds packed in long pods are ground into flour to make cakes and are also used to brew a strong drink, while the bran remaining from the flour grinding process makes a refreshing non-alcoholic beverage.

Far to the north, the tropical and sub-tropical river systems with their networks of streams and swamps amid dense vegetation are the habitat of many varieties of snakes and of alligators. The snub-nosed alligator, or *yacaré ñato*, is an interesting example which, apart from its diet of crustaceans, frogs, toads, snakes, fish, snails and rodents, also swallows stones from the riverbed. It is believed these stones serve as ballast, helping it to maintain equilibrium and facilitate immersion and navigation. It has a huge mouth, powerful jaws and sharp teeth, as well as thick armoured hide and a very dangerous tail which it uses effectively as an additional weapon.

The decline in numbers due to excessive hunting for commercial purposes, basically for handbags and shoes, has led to serious disruptions in the ecological chain, not the least being the appearance of the terrifying razor-toothed *piraña* fish in the rivers, even reaching as far south as Buenos Aires. Previously it was rare outside Brazilian rivers, precisely because alligators and crocodiles were the natural control.

Several kinds of monkeys inhabit the tropical forests. The howlers or *carayá* are one of the varieties found in greatest numbers. According to a Guaraní legend, the *carayás* were once men but when the earth took fire after colliding with the sun the monkeys, instead of seeking refuge in the rivers, climbed to the treetops where they have remained ever since, singed and shrunken by the fire.

Another inhabitant of these regions is the tapir which perhaps was intended to evolve into some other animal as it is described as having a body like a pig, small sunken eyes like a rhinoceros, a miniature elephant's trunk and a mane like a horse. In spite of its rough appearance and corpulence, weighing about 500 lb, it is very agile. In Guaraní astronomy, the Milky Way is called the 'Road of the Tapir'. The world's largest rodent, the carpincho, is also to be found in the area. It weighs more than 100 lb and stands about thirty inches high. It is inoffensive, reddish brown in colour and easily tamed. It is clumsy on land but swims well and can remain submerged a long time without difficulty.

Still subsisting in the tropical jungle is the panther, known here as the *yaguareté*. Its hide is brilliant reddish-yellow with black spots of different sizes, while some extremely scarce, entirely black panthers also exist.

Further south in the vast Mesopotamian marshlands, among the tall grass and rushes, lives a shy nocturnal creature with a rather complicated double-barrel name and the appearance of a fox on stilts. It is the *aguará-guazú*. It has the sharp angular face of a fox, large ears and thick, reddish fur especially over its shoulders, for which reason it is sometimes referred to as a maned wolf.

The tropical forests abound in a great variety of birds, perhaps the most striking one is the toucan. It is known as the 'clown of the jungle', restless, noisy, sociable, boisterous. The enormous, brightly coloured beak is really very light-weight and has a serrated edge which it uses to chop up larger size fruit. It is voracious and omniverous and though its diet is principally fruit and seeds, it also eats the eggs and chicks of other birds, insects and reptiles. Its harsh call sounds like the croaking of a frog. Toucans often 'sing' together in strident chorus, with beaks clacking and heads swaying. The din they make increases considerably, for some reason, when it rains.

The Andes mountains, marking the western limits of Argentina, stretch from the equatorial north to Tierra del Fuego in the south. They are the home of the condor, which could be regarded as the king of South American birds. It has a striking appearance, naked head and neck, white fluffy collar, a large body covered with black plumage edged with white, while its full wingspan reaches more than three yards. A symbol of the mighty Andes, it is not really the terrifying creature it is so often represented to be. It is quite unable to carry off its prey in its talons as it needs to run a considerable distance in order to become successfully airborne due to its great weight and size. It feeds exclusively on carrion and, as is the case with many other birds and animals, its reputation as a raider is unjustified.

Ranging all over the length and breadth of Argentina, in different sizes and colours is the hummingbird, in fact it is found throughout the whole Western Hemisphere from Canada to Tierra del Fuego. It is an intensely active creature and the very high consumption of energy its extraordinary flight demands, means it must take in every day about half its weight in sugars and double its weight in water, nectar and insects. They are the only birds which can fly sideways, backwards and remain suspended in the air without ceasing wing movement. The first known chroniclers initially had doubts about the nature of the hummingbirds. It was proposed that they underwent a curious metamorphosis: from the egg a worm emerged to be transformed later into a mosquito and then into a butterfly. After a while it would reach adult stage in the form of a hummingbird.

For the Guaraní Indians the hummingbird is a divine messenger and they consider it watches over young children. When they had to leave a child alone, they would place bunches of flowers beside it so

Where The Devil Lost His Poncho

that the hummingbird would stay near, watching. They also believed that when a person dies the soul takes refuge in a flower where it is found by the hummingbird, which takes it to Paradise. The Mapuches of northern Patagonia, on the other hand, regarded it as a bad omen, but in the far south the Onas of Tierra del Fuego looked upon it as the symbol of a small but valiant personage.

One summer evening in our Buenos Aires garden I had a very happy encounter with a hummingbird. It was that magic moment when the sun has just set and for the following fifteen minutes the light in some way intensifies all colours: red flowers seem to take fire, yellows and orange glow, white blossoms are almost luminous and the greens become vibrant. The heat of the day was still great and I was watering a flower bed with a strong arc of fine spray, when a many-coloured hummingbird began to dart in and out of the water. It continued for perhaps a full minute as I watched, keeping absolutely motionless and enraptured at the privilege of sharing an instant with this little, jewel-like creature.

The family. Buenos Aires 1963

Also abundant all over the country are the parrots which in some parts reach plague proportions. The plain green Patagonian cousins of the gorgeous birds from the jungle are rather drab in comparison and live up in the mountains. When they come down in winter in noisy, swooping flocks to the lower slopes, it is said to be a sign of imminent snowstorms. Local ski fanatics, watching the weather anxiously for snow when winter begins, happily regard the appearance of the parrots as headline news.

Typical of the more arid Andean scene are the South American cousins of the camel: the llama, vicuña, alpaca and guanaco. The llama and the alpaca are now only found in captivity, having been domesticated many centuries ago and of the four, the llama is the largest. The vicuña, the smallest, is also slender and agile, particularly on steep slopes and in snow and is able to gallop at over thirty miles an hour. It is found exclusively at high altitudes where the climate tends to be arid and cold. It provides one of the most sought-after fibres in the world and the exceptional quality of its wool led to intense persecution and slaughter. Since it can tolerate only four shearings in its lifetime, it was customary to kill the animal instead. Fine and resistant, this wool provides very light but very warm garments, although a single poncho requires the wool of four vicuñas.

The guanaco, slightly larger than the vicuña, is able to adapt easily to a wide variety of climate and terrain. It is plentiful and widespread in the whole sub-continent and it provided the Indians of earlier centuries with valuable elements of daily life: wool, meat, hides, bones and sinews. The guanaco, unlike sheep and cattle, does not erode the land where it grazes, partly because its feet are padded instead of hoofed and partly because its teeth are so formed that it does not bite the blades of vegetation right to soil level but leaves a small portion to regenerate.

There are several projects in operation to see if the guanaco can be profitably exploited in place of sheep on severely overgrazed land. It is frequently seen in the company of vicuñas and ostriches. Like the vicuña it is extremely agile and scrambles surefootedly over rough, steep land. The Ona tribe of Tierra del Fuego regarded it as the most important animal in their lives. Today the Onas are but a memory while the guanacos still exist. In this case, the animals have been more fortunate than the human aborigine.

Returning to the Province of Buenos Aires, its fertility and warm climate are appreciated not only by the farmers and ranchers but also by the many amateur gardeners. Semi-tropical and even tropical plants grow very well, with some protection from the occasional winter frosts. One example in my suburban garden was a vigorous plant of Strelitzia. Its astonishing flowers resembling blue and orange birds in full flight grew profusely for months on end and I never tired of them. Flowering bushes and roses were very rewarding, too, but I regarded the trees as the year-round wonder. In one corner an old gnarled mimosa became a cascade of gold against a background of dark pines before the winter ended, to be followed by the pink and white of various prunus trees. Myrtle, gynko, red-thorn, Japanese maple, tulip-tree, the New Zealand bottle-brush, green and yellow acacias, buddleia, catalpa and silvery eucalyptus and finally an exquisite old magnolia, vied with each other for our admiration.

And when darkness hid the lovely summer garden, the fireflies would appear in their hundreds, providing an indescribably beautiful display of flashing and darting lights. Usually at the same time, however, the garden would also be full of bloodthirsty mosquitos, so it was advisable to watch the firefly ballet from behind the window netting.

Nevertheless, it was impossible to spend too much time admiring the garden because meanwhile the multitudinous insect population never rested. Among the non-beneficial varieties the most relentless of them all is probably the large black ant, insatiable, inexterminable. I had tried all the advertised ant-killers, usually with some initial success but it seems the ants rapidly develop immunity to poisons.

One supposedly infallible product consisted of small pink pellets which had to be spread near the entrance to the nest or along the main ant 'highways' which cut across the lawn like autobahns. Apparently, some sweet substance in those grains attracted the ants and they carried them away enthusiastically into their silos. In the course of the night the granules would begin to release a lethal gas due to the temperature and humidity of the antheap and the inhabitants would be asphyxiated.

The first time this was tried the result appeared to be the

annihilation of the colony but there must have been an odd survivor or two because when it became evident some time later that the ants were on the war path again, they ignored the pink 'candies'. They had obviously been warned. At one point I selected a large ant which was returning to base with a choice slice of rose leaf. I removed the leaf with tweezers and exchanged it for a small granule, which the ant accepted. But instead of continuing homeward, it turned round and hurried off in the opposite direction and presumably dumped the gas bomb somewhere else.

Following suggestions by organic gardening enthusiasts, generally regarded in those days as cranks, and guided by an incomparable U.S. magazine dedicated to Organic Gardening and Farming, I changed my tactics. I planted onions and garlic among the roses and at other strategic points and sprayed flower-beds and vegetable plots with a potent solution of chopped peppers, onions, garlic and aromatic herbs in plain water. This caused some facetious remarks by friends and neighbours and my solution became known as *chimi-churri* which is the name of a spicy dressing used in Argentina on steaks and happens to include the same ingredients as my ant-deterrent. The *chimi-churri* certainly did not exterminate the ants but it kept them well away from the plants.

Since then I have been an enthusiast of organic methods of cultivation and of combatting garden pests and plant diseases. My inspiration came mostly from the magazine referred to above, published by the Rodale Institute of Emmaus, Pennsylvania, in the U.S., a research organization which has pioneered and expounded the organic gospel for over fifty years. The founder, J.I. Rodale, was undoubtedly a man of great vision and courage, who was succeeded by his son Robert Rodale, equally dedicated to reversing the insane destruction of Nature, of the very planet.

In Argentina, plague proportions similar to those of the rabbit in Australia exist with the European hare and the common sparrow and, in a general way, with the weeds and bugs which invade new territories as they accompany the normal traffic of goods. According to the ecologists, every invader – animal or vegetable – which successfully gains a foothold in a territory causes the extinction of up to four other local species. It is now too late to cry over the ecological disruption and attempt to deport all the unwelcome immigrants.

It seems that by now the general public is aware of the dangers facing the planet yet politicians and industrialists do not appear to have registered the message in all its crudity. At the beginning of the seventies it was evident that the predominant trend towards urban life in most of the world would be too strong for the relatively few people preoccupied with ecological and related predicaments. Nevertheless, concern over the environment spread notably and even the most hardened city-dweller began to express alarm over huge oil spills or devastation of tropical forests. It is imperative that authorities everywhere stop shirking the issue and get down to taking the necessary measures and countermeasures, although it may already be too late.

In this connection, the world owes a great debt of gratitude to Rachel Carson, yet the ordinary citizen who is up to date with the names and absurdities of movie stars and sports champions would probably be unable to say who she was. At the time she published her famous book, *Silent Spring*, in 1962, the industrialized countries were enthusiastically surging ahead with their scientific and technological accomplishments that simultaneously were devastating the planet with waste and pollution.

The book, denouncing this destruction, fell like a bombshell. It was violently refuted and execrated by the corporations thriving on the multitude of chemical products which were supposed to solve so many of humanity's problems. But her message fell on fertile ground also and helped to stimulate into positive action the growing body of observers anxiously witnessing the deterioration which threatened to ravage the natural life of the earth. Rachel Carson deserves very high recognition as a benefactor of humanity and environmentalists and all other nature lovers would do well to see that her name becomes familiar to the public everywhere.

By good luck rather than good management, Argentina has so far been spared much of the irreversible damage suffered by the industrialized nations. It is to be fervently hoped that, with the excesses and mistakes committed by those nations and plainly visible as regards the use and abuse of resources, Argentina will have learned

Flora and Fauna, among other things

how to avoid such disasters.

When the red European deer was introduced into the western pampas for 'sporting' purposes, it appeared a good idea to sportsmen and completely unimportant to non-sportsmen. In the course of time, the deer escaped from the hunting grounds and soon found their way to the Andean forests where they thrived remarkably. The puma was their only likely enemy but this had been hunted into decline by sheep and cattle ranchers and did not make much impact on the rapid reproduction of the imported species. Unfortunately, this red deer has contributed to the near extinction of local deer, notably the *huemul* and the *pudú-pudú*. These are very small creatures, the latter barely larger than a terrier. It is said that these two species can still be found in the high mountain where the red deer - and dogs - do not reach, while promising results have been achieved in breeding the *pudú-pudú* in experimental stations.

In Tierra del Fuego a serious problem arose when someone blithely released a few Canadian beavers into the rivers of the densely wooded southern part of the island. The beavers went ahead energetically to construct their damns and wherever they went they drowned sizable areas of forest. Since Tierra del Fuego is an island, thus practically isolated from eventual reinforcements from the continental mainland where the beavers are said to exist in the south of Chile, it is hoped that over the years Nature herself will find the natural way to create a new ecological balance, particularly by keeping down the beaver population to its minimum for subsistence. According to ecologists and geographers, all research about the flora and fauna as well as the biogeography of the Island must now of necessity be divided into B.B. and A.B. Before the Beaver and After the Beaver.

The overwhelming importance of trees in restoring much of the ecological balance and improving quality of life the world over is no longer doubted. Their capacity for purifying city air and simultaneously beautifying urban drabness is little short of miraculous. Away from the city, they are essential to combat erosion, limit flooding, provide a habitat for innumerable creatures and, in short, they are of unending benefit to mankind both physically and spiritually. It would seem that mankind has been the greatest enemy of the trees. If great forests remain upon the earth, it is probably because man has not yet managed to devastate them. The surge of interest in ecology has not occurred a moment too soon. If every child could be taught to love and admire the trees there would be no need to fear their wholesale destruction in the future.

Some years ago the United Nations University published the astonishing story about the 'planter of trees', Elzéard Bouffier, as told by Jean Giono.

Giono related that in the summer of 1913 he was tramping through a lonely region of France where the Alps descend into Provence. One day he came upon the ruins of a deserted mountain village. All around was desolation, swept by searing hot winds and he could find no water anywhere, so he continued for several hours more, hoping that somewhere he would find a spring. Instead, he met a solitary shepherd with a few sheep, who gave him water from his gourd and took him to his cabin to spend the night. In the course of the evening the shepherd brought out a bag and spilled the contents on to the table. They were acorns. He began to inspect them carefully and selected about 100.

The next day before setting out with his flock, the shepherd soaked the acorns in a bucket of water and Giono noted he was carrying an iron pole about a metre and a half long instead of the usual shepherd's crook. Eventually, he left the sheep in a small pasture, guarded by his dog and he invited Giono to accompany him to the higher part of the hill. Once there, he began to stick his pole into the ground and in each resulting hole he placed an acorn and covered it with soil. Giono, greatly intrigued, plied him with questions. Was the land his?

No, he did not know whose land it was, perhaps it belonged to the local authority.

How long had he been planting acorns?

More than three years.

How many had he planted?

About 100,000 and 20,000 had germinated.

He figured that about half of the saplings might be lost to rodents or the inscrutable designs of Providence but 10,000 would be left growing where before there was desolation. He told Giono that he was 55, his name was Elzéard Bouffier, that he had had a farm in the lowlands but after losing his only son and his wife, he had retired to a life of solitude with his sheep and the dog. It had seemed to him that this land was dying for lack of trees and he had decided to try to do something. Apart from his acorns he had planted a nursery of beech saplings and was intending to include silver birch as well.

Giono returned to the scene at the end of World War I. He was almost speechless at the spectacle before him. The oaks planted in 1910 were all of six feet tall, a forest eleven kilometres long and three kilometres at the widest point. Elzéard Bouffier told him he had meanwhile switched from sheep to bees and had a hundred hives and only four sheep; apparently, the sheep were a constant menace to the saplings. The beeches were now shoulder high and there were beautiful groups of silver birches in the lower parts where he had rightly suspected that there was humidity close to the surface. It would seem that Nature had then set off a chain reaction. Water was running in streams that had long been dry, the wind had dispersed other seeds. With the return of the water, bullrushes, willows, pastures and flowers had appeared.

In 1933 a forest warden reached Bouffier's cabin and notified him that it was forbidden to light a fire in the open air to avoid the danger of destroying this 'natural forest'. Bouffier did not enlighten him and two years later officials from the Forestry Bureau, a Deputy and some technicians came to inspect the natural forest. It was placed under State protection and the production of charcoal was prohibited. Fortunately, the forest emerged practically unscathed from World War II, mostly due to its inaccessibility.

Giono returned in June 1945 and the ruined village of 1913 had become transformed into a thriving though tiny community set in a resuscitated countryside. Bouffier was then 87. Giono refers to him as one of God's athletes. The constant, peaceful labour, walking incessantly in the invigorating mountain air, frugality of life and above all, serenity of spirit, had given him health in abundance. The benefits of Bouffier's mountain forest spread widely, overflowing into the plains below, bringing new fertility and health to a widespread population. It is estimated that over 100,000 persons owe the basis of their happiness to Elzéard Bouffier, who died peacefully in 1947.

It was very gratifying to learn through the *Organic Gardening* magazine of February 1991 that the American Forestry Association's Global Re-leaf Campaign has instituted the Jean Giono Award for honouring outstanding citizen tree planters.

Bouffier's name has certainly not become a household word, his story is not common knowledge, he seems to have been relegated to the same public oblivion as Rachel Carson. Can nothing be done to draw urgent attention to the example of people like Bouffier, Rachel Carson and the Rodales and galvanise into action irresponsible bureaucrats, industrialists and other leading figures who are seemingly incapable of realizing how little time is left to save the life of the planet?

No account of Argentina would be complete without reference to the creole horse, *el caballo criollo*, which could be considered the outstanding representative of Argentina fauna. As described and demonstrated by my old hero, Tschiffely, it is incomparable in endurance, the result of centuries of natural selection in an environment that was often extremely hostile. The creole is the descendant of the few Spanish horses abandoned after the sack of a little village called Buenos Aires and the massacre of its inhabitants in 1560 by the Indians. It stands only about fifteen hands high, is sturdy, stocky and its hide is often sandy-coloured though there are many shades and variations. It may not be especially handsome when compared to the European or Arab riding horse but, as Tschiffely insisted, handsome is as handsome does. It is bred today in significant numbers and in accordance with the Creole Stud Book standards.

As a polo pony it has been proved to be one of the best. One ranch dedicated exclusively to the raising of polo ponies is an example of a little-known, profitable activity which presumably earns considerable foreign currency for the country. On this ranch hundreds of creoles are reared and trained permanently in polo and a heterogeneous group of polo players from all over the world can usually be found there, training and practising daily. Most of the 'students' return home with several splendidly prepared horses. It seems that the owner of the ranch began exporting creoles for polo but it was not so easy to meet the demand. He is said to have hedge-hopped over the Province of Buenos Aires in his little aeroplane, looking for likely animals and, on spotting some, would land on a handy road or field and close the deal there and then with the surprised owner.

This creole horse was the gaucho's most valued possession. One of the rather stereotyped symbols of Argentina along with tangos and beefsteaks, the gaucho no longer exists in his original form. Today the term is applied to ranch and farmhands who work with cattle and horses.

In the early days, however, the gaucho was the stubbornly independent, wandering cowboy of the plains who drove the vast herds of wild cattle and disdained the luxuries or even the simple commodities of urban civilization. He regarded Authority as repression and servitude and followed his own lonely trail, or joined in the conflicts of local political bosses, known as caudillos, against the ruling power. The gaucho was of mixed Indian and Spanish blood, usually the offspring of the numerous white women taken captive in the violent raids on settlements by Indians on the warpath, as well as of Indian women abused by the whites. Their situation seemed to arouse none of the sympathy felt for the white captives which, of course, is consistent with the contempt for the 'inferior breeds', prevalent until recently as one of the facts of life and far from eradicated as yet.

All the gaucho needed was his horse, a sheepskin saddle, a knife and a *boleadora*. This latter is a device consisting of three rawhide thongs joined together and weighted with stones which is thrown so as to wrap around the legs of the animal being hunted, causing it to fall. Anything else was superfluous and his greatest shame was to be without a horse and to have to walk. The twilight for the gaucho came with the wire fence which in the late nineteenth century began to divide up the wide open spaces and restricted the wanderings of cattle and humans alike. The gauchos continued to work with cattle but they became dependants, employees or mere peons of the landowners.

The real gaucho story has been immortalized in the epic poem 'Martín Fierro' by José Hernández, which has become part of the linguistic fabric of Argentina. It is as quotable as *Hamlet* and could be regarded as a very early protest song, in its compassionate description of a long-suffering sector of Argentine society.

Literary production of all kinds in the Argentine is prolific indeed, in fact Latin America as a whole is remarkable for the vigour and originality of its writers and poets. Latin America naturally includes Brazil with its flourishing literary production in Portuguese. If the production of Spain is considered, it is apparent that literature in the Spanish language represents a formidable cultural contribution yet it is mostly unknown to the rest of the world dominated by English-language publications. Obviously, good translations are required but it appears that the translator is regarded in general as a low-level office hack and it is rare that a publisher willingly pays even moderately adequate fees to ensure competent work.

Translation is not just a case of knowing two languages and switching from one to the other, like a machine. The richer the translator's cultural background and the greater his sensitivity to literary expression, the more acceptable will his version be in another language. Borges and a few long-established Latin American authors were able to arrange for impeccable translations of their work but the tendency is to rely on needy bilinguals who are not too scrupulous about their qualifications, who have to keep their bids low and meet a tough deadline.

Language, after all, is a fascinating subject and in our bilingual immigrant condition it was ever-present as a problem. Back in Argentina, the children began the normal process of making friends and going to school. It didn't seem to matter that they could speak no Spanish or had forgotten any they may have acquired once at a very early age. In a matter of a month they were ready to drop English as unnecessary and from then on till the end of their teens, I struggled to make them realize the advantage of keeping up English, of taking it in painlessly without tears at home. Evidently, some rubbed off on them or they maybe absorbed it by a kind of osmosis before they finally accepted it as worthwhile. All those years I stubbornly spoke to them in English and they answered as stubbornly in Spanish, to the amusement and surprise of any visitors who happened to be present.

It is said that immigrants' children tend to be very determined to figure as native citizens, that they dislike being heard speaking the

Flora and Fauna, among other things

parents' mother tongue, that they are highly embarrassed by the errors and mispronunciations of their parents when speaking the newly-learned language. I can testify that the latter is a sore point. One of the bothersome problems of Spanish concerns remembering noun genders, which does not arise in English. Years ago, my husband referred to *la mapa* instead of *el mapa* and the children regarded this as so amusing that he has never been allowed to forget it. It is a reasonable enough mistake for any foreigner to make but it will presumably follow him to the grave.

On the other hand, Argentines are very patient and helpful with the foreigner who is trying to converse and, in the process, is mangling their language unmercifully. I have noticed that the English and Americans show no such patience and make little allowance for linguistic difficulties. They also assume it as one of the facts of life that English is understood and spoken 'everywhere'. My own observation, however, is that even where it is taught in secondary schools as an obligatory subject, comparatively few people seem able to hold a simple conversation and as for writing English correctly, this is extremely rare even, for example, among professionals and others using English for their research or business.

English names are frequently found in Argentina. Many towns and locations so named are a legacy of early settlers and often of the railway system built by the British. Nowadays American predominance in international business and industry no doubt accounts for many other English words in daily use. However, a characteristic of the Argentines is to pronounce foreign words, according to Spanish pronunciation and accentuation rules. It is not the result of ignorance because it occurs at all levels.

One of our first acquaintances here told us he worked for the North American company Feeresstonay, meaning Firestone, while the most popular soft drink at that time was called Croosh, though of course spelled Crush. Somewhere in the corn belt we once came upon a signpost to James Craik and we checked at the service station that the place was known as Hammays Cryke.

The contrast with the custom in Chile is notable because for some reason the Chileans carefully pronounce foreign names as correctly as possible. In the case of English, it could be a reflection of the attitude of the two countries towards the 'Big Brothers' in the north. The Chileans normally maintain friendly relations with the U.S. and Britain, while Argentina has always been instinctively antagonistic towards the U.S. and traditionally not too enthusiastic about the U.K. So the unwillingness of Argentines to give the proper English pronunciation could be a conscious or subconscious expression of some kind of hostility or disdain, or maybe just plain cussedness.

If Argentine literature is not universally well known, the tango has certainly travelled far and wide. It is the most famous expression of Argentine popular music though it represents only a portion of the country's abundant musical activity. It is known as 'city music' or urban folklore as opposed to the many regional types of rhythm and melody. The tango with its strident music accompanied by often bitter, tragic or ironic words, reflected the frustration and harshness of life in the crowded slums where it was born in the late nineteenth century. Thousands of immigrants lived in those slums and their poverty and struggles must have been intensified by the anguish of being so far from the homeland.

The vigour and originality of the tango in its native Buenos Aires make it totally unlike the respectable ballroom tango known in Europe, for example. It took me several years of living in Argentina and absorbing the country's particular atmosphere, history and character, to become accustomed to tangos and to enjoy them. Across the years there have been different phases: sadly melodious, brashly rhythmical and nowadays, discordantly modern. Judging by the amount of tango music broadcast everywhere, it seems to have long overcome the decline that set in when, in the fifties, North American rhythms threatened to sweep all local music out of existence. It is certainly an achievement that the city of Buenos Aires should have been able to distil the essence of its *weltanschauung* into a musical, artistic expression that became world-famous and continues to thrive.

The supreme, unchallenged interpreter of the tango is still Carlos Gardel, who died sixty years ago in a tragic aeroplane accident in Colombia. Modern recording technology has been able to recapture the beauty of his voice from scratchy old gramophone records. With his affability and charm, it is no wonder the Argentines have enshrined

Flora and Fauna, among other things

him among their immortals. It is said that the great Caruso marvelled at the unusual range and purity of Gardel's voice, and told him: 'Truly you have tears in your throat.' Even trivial words or unpretentious melodies became enhanced and meaningful when sung by Gardel.

The late Jorge A. Sábato, a prominent Argentine expert in nuclear problems, was also a great admirer of Gardel and in one of his articles in the newspaper, *La Opinión*, in June 1975, he refers to the surprising popularity of Gardel and the tango in the whole of Latin America:

'I suspect in the first place that his success in the rest of Latin America, then and now, owes much to the fact that Gardel was the first Latin American to win world fame thanks to those three magical inventions – the crystal set radio, the handwound gramophone and sound cinema with talking and singing – which carried him to all latitudes.'

Sábato goes on to refer to his local popularity.

'I also suspect that his success among us, then and now, is linked to the fact that he is the Man of Buenos Aires, through whom the inhabitant of this city, seeking his own authentic identity, inevitably encounters Gardel, the key protagonist of the tango which is the most genuine popular expression of the solitude of the city-dweller.'

Curiously enough, Gardel was a fellow student of Ceferino Namuncurá in 1901 in the Pius IV College of Buenos Aires. For some reason this convergence of the two figures of the widest popular devotion in subsequent years is not generally known. Pablo Fermín Oreja in his book, *Desde la Cúpula*, contrasts the circumstances of their youth: Ceferino, the son of a legendary ruler of the Pampas and who barely remembered his mother; and Gardel, born in France, father unknown, and whose mother made a humble living for herself and her son as a washerwoman in a working-class district of Buenos Aires.

Argentine devotion to Gardel has been seen by some short-term visitors to the country as further proof of the morbid necrophilic tendency affecting Argentines as a whole. This is nonsense. All humans have to die sometime so it is obvious that local heroes and anti-heroes alike will be dead eventually. If their admirers remain faithful to the memory of Carlos Gardel or Eva Perón or General San Martín, it is no more necrophilic than North American admiration of Lincoln or British reverence for Nelson.

Other regions of Argentina have well-defined, attractive styles known as folklore music. The people of the great river systems in the warm littoral produce unmistakable, harmonious songs. There is a strong influence from the Guaraní natives who learned to become accomplished musicians at the time of the Jesuit Reductions in the seventeenth century. The extraordinary experiment of the 'Reductions' consisted of the construction of self-supporting agricultural and educational units, to teach the Guaraní Indians, along with evangelization and protection from raiding Brazilian slavers, all kinds of crafts, including cultivation of the land, carpentry and construction.

The Guaranís proved to be gifted carvers in wood and stone and the exuberant baroque prevailing at the time took on new vigour in the sub-tropical Mesopotamia of what is now Argentine, Paraguayan and Brazilian territory. The Guaraní language continues to be widely spoken in those regions and this has presumably helped maintain the identity of the race, without seeming to have hindered integration into the present-day nations. Their songs are lyrical and melodious with an appropriately flowing, river-like rhythm and are interpreted most authentically on the so-called Paraguayan harp.

Further north and west, where Argentina meets Bolivia on the high Andean plateaux, the music and instruments are totally different. They are probably fairly well known abroad due to the wide diffusion given in recent years to music of the Andes played on reed pipes, such as the quena. The lively carnival themes are highly attractive and reflect the few days of colour and laughter that brighten the harsh existence of these long-suffering people of the Altiplano.

A large variety of dances and rhythms popular in the whole country and not necessarily confined to or typical of one region, characterizes the rest of Argentine folk music. They include the

Flora and Fauna, among other things

milonga, the chamamé, cueca, gato and zamba, this latter being very different from the Brazilian samba. While there are many professional groups of musicians, some of international repute, probably every community in the country, from a few lonely ranchhands, to villages, towns and cities, has its *peña folklórica* or group of amateur performers, usually with guitar or accordion as accompanying instruments. Every year the town of Cosquín in the Córdoba hills stages a great national festival, with individuals and groups competing for fame and fortune. Out of this festival come the new material and new voices and it is indeed a demonstration of the vitality and popularity of the folk music.

Argentina has produced throughout its short history a significant number of composers and performers of classical music. One of the first native composers was Alberto Williams, of Welsh descent, who introduced a strong flavour of Argentine rhythms and style into his compositions. At the present time there are several exceptional concert pianists, both men and women, while other instrumentalists appear regularly on international circuits. A pioneer group of chamber music players, the Camerata Bariloche, originating in the Fundación Bariloche referred to in the next chapter, reached the highest levels of interpretation and evidently led the way to the establishment of numerous other groups, both orchestral and choral.

Sad to say, Argentina has suffered from a very unfortunate political image abroad resulting from the clash between those twin scourges of humanity, extremisms of the Left and the Right, against a background of political mismanagement within the framework of brutal military dictatorships. Its 180 years as an independent nation have been punctuated with high hopes and deep deceptions, with generosity and wretched frauds, with abuse from within and from without. In the 1920s its standard of living was comparable with the most prosperous European countries but after 1930, when the constitutional process was interrupted by the first of a series of *coups d'état* alternating with brief periods of democracy, there followed a discouraging story of marches and countermarches in developing the country's resources, of hopeful starts and disappointing failures. Some interesting projects, like the National Library, took decades to materialize, or even to reach the stage of turning the first sod.

Argentines continually lamented their apparent inability to 'take-off' and participate successfully in the advances of modern times, as they undoubtedly seem to have both the human and natural resources to do so. As far as human resources are concerned, the general consensus is that she is decidedly underpopulated and, worse still, distribution of the population is heavily lopsided, with a third crowded into the megalopolis stretching from La Plata, just south of Buenos Aires city, to Rosario, 300 miles up the River Paraná. Patagonia which represents nearly one-third of Argentine territory has only five per cent of the total inhabitants. Although Patagonia is traditionally considered to be underpopulated, stagnated and forgotten, it would appear that this is not quite the case. The existence of great distances from one small township to another with apparently not a soul in between, has probably led to a misreading of the situation and failing to realize that wherever conditions exist for human habitation, someone will be found there.

Periodically, serious suggestions are put forward (mostly by people who know little about the region at first-hand) for projects like diverting rivers and irrigating the steppes and making them fertile and productive. Such schemes are totally unfeasible for many reasons, too technical to deal with here, and certainly it would seem quite unnecessary to attempt to make available more land when the valleys and other areas already irrigated and bursting with fertility only produce a fraction of their potentiality or are even unable to sell their merchandise profitably. The conclusion is that Patagonia is not under-populated but that it has just about the population it can support. I suppose that must sound like downright heresy to many, but I have this information on the best authority from local researchers profoundly involved in experience and study of Patagonia.

One of the proposals of former President Alfonsín, elected in 1983 on the return to constitutional government, was to transfer the Federal Capital from Buenos Aires to Patagonia, specifically to the twin cities of Viedma and Carmen de Patagones, situated respectively on the south and north banks near the mouth of the River Negro. It had long been recognized that the overcrowded megalopolis spreading like a cancer from the city of Buenos Aires over the conurban towns

Flora and Fauna, among other things

and along the banks of the Plate and the Paraná, was paralyzing the rest of the country, becoming ever more inefficient and unmanageable, straining services to their limits and being at the mercy of destabilizing activities. In other words, it suffers the typical maladies of the outsize cities of present times.

So Alfonsín wanted to cut the Gordian knot of invested interests, political jealousies and inertias, taking the nation by surprise. For Patagonia it was an unbelievably happy surprise, suddenly lighting up the scene which had seemed destined to continuing stagnation on the periphery of the nation.

As might be imagined, reactions in Buenos Aires were mixed, with a strong dose of disbelief and ironic comments. 'Viedma? Where's that?'

Alfonsín's challenge: 'To the South, to the Sea, to the Cold', caused some acute shudders among the less imaginative, more pusillanimous spirits and although the transfer was approved by Congress, it is presently shelved, particularly in view of the enormous cost of the undertaking. Perhaps if the economy continues on an even keel and advances satisfactorily, the project might be refloated.

Viedma was founded in 1779 on the right bank of the River Negro but a few months later the settlers had to move to the left bank as the result of a devastating flood. The second settlement received the name of Carmen de Patagones and subsequently the two towns grew up together. Meanwhile in 1827, Carmen de Patagones was the scene of a vital battle when a Brazilian fleet of warships attempted to capture the town. The whole population - soldiers, farmers, Indians, ranchers, shopkeepers, tradesmen and a sprinkling of foreigners - enthusiastically joined forces and were able to throw out the invaders.

One of the foreigners was an English merchant navy captain, Edmund Elsegood, of whom little is known. A small monument by the side of the River Negro close to the town perpetuates his memory. The inscription reads to the effect that: 'Serving as liaison with the Commander Luís Piedrabuena, he helped consolidate Argentine sovereignty in Patagonia'.

When provincial limits were defined, the River Negro marked the division between the provinces of Buenos Aires and Rio Negro, Patagones belonging to the former and Viedma to the latter. Eventually,

Viedma was named the capital of the province and acquired a new dynamism as a result, while Patagones retained its colonial, peaceful atmosphere. If these two cities should ever become the base for integrating Patagonia into its rightful place, it will help to put into practice the federal system which up to now has existed mainly in theory.

The return to democracy in 1983 brought with it profound confrontations, such as the trial of the military leaders for serious crimes committed in their so-called war against communist-inspired terrorism and the refusal of the Armed Forces to admit they had gone too far in the repression.

Altogether, President Alfonsín had to face thirteen general strikes trumped up by the hostile General Trades Union, three military rebellions of dangerous implications, as well as the expected harassment by Peronists and other smaller opposition parties. He was unable to dominate the economy consumed by never-ending inflation. This had been with us almost continually since the sixties and even before that. We had grown accustomed to it and learned how to live with it, as long as it stayed within 'manageable levels'.

The time came, unfortunately, when the upward spiral started to soar and, in accordance with a well-known comment, 'prices went up by the elevator while wages went by the stairs'. Every now and then the current economic wizard would lop a few zeros off the peso, change the currency denomination and hope for the best. One of the most serious climaxes came when we found ourselves with million-peso notes and handling hundreds of thousands for everyday purchases.

The cash registers and computers had no room for more zeros so a new currency, the austral, was invented fixed at slightly above par with the dollar. We lost all the zeros again and thus ended our ephemeral experience of being millionaires. It was rather a shock to find one's salary reduced overnight from, say, fifteen million pesos to something like 95 australs.

Over the years the debasement of the currency was enormous and came close to wiping out the once fairly prosperous Argentine middle class. Sad to say, the austral soon went the same way as its predecessors and, in spite of it seeming at one time that this policy had put a stop to inflation, the necessary stern economic measures and firm political support of the Economy Minister's audacious measures, were never applied and six months before the completion of Alfonsín's legal term of office, his government ended in a frightful acceleration of hyper-inflation which threatened to plunge the country into complete disintegration.

That was the first time I experienced a real feeling of panic about the inflation. It was the same sensation I had known years ago when, bathing with the children in Mar del Plata, I suddenly felt the undertow threatening to sweep us out to sea. We had been able to get back to the beach and in fact we were only a few yards from the shore but I have never forgotten the shock.

In a case of hyper-inflation the framework of daily life dissolves. For instance, one day I bought a bus ticket to go to La Pampa the following day, but when I was boarding the bus I had to pay an extra charge because the price had shot up in the interval. As for the return journey, the price was by then nearly double. This pattern occurred with everything: newspapers, food, properties, and in trade and commerce it was often impossible for the storekeeper to learn the replacement cost of the articles. So much so, that many businesses just shut up shop.

In these catastrophic circumstances the new president, Carlos Saúl Menem, took office, to the exultation of the Peronists and the dismay of everyone else. It soon became apparent, however, that Menem intended to ditch the worn-out populist theories that had helped bring the country to the edge of the abyss. In other words, Menem had opted for the market economy of capitalism, judging it to be the only alternative if the country was ever to recover. He found he had sufficient support from the general public to go ahead with his Argentine *perestroika* but, naturally enough, many Peronists felt betrayed and the Radicals of Alfonsín were outraged. Parliament often dragged its feet over vital legislation, the military frequently rattled their sabres ominously though ineffectively, the once-powerful trades union organization split in two and is now no longer the 'backbone of Peronism'.

So far, Menem has been more than a match for his detractors, especially those of the mass media, who insist that the prodigious recovery and stabilization of the foundering company, has been achieved at too high a social cost. Be that as it may, the social cost of the previous policies was infinitely greater and I am convinced that Menem has earned the gratitude of millions of Argentines for his audacity and skill in setting the nation on a most auspicious course.

Cleaning up the economy meant drastic reduction of the asphyxiating bureaucracy with its incredible overload of personnel and corrupt practices, bribery at all levels and widespread inefficiency. As an example, the State Oil Enterprise, Y.P.F., was the only large oil company in the world which operated deep in the red and all the other State concerns were similarly bleeding the country white. The need to uproot and end corruption is probably the government's most urgent objective but it is clearly comparable to cleaning the Augean stables and will take more than a local Hercules to do the job.

In all this turmoil, the democracy born in 1983 has been severely tried and tested, gathering strength from each new attack. Argentina, inimically weakened by an interminable crisis, needed a vision of the future which is not grey and sombre or, alternatively, apocalyptic. It needs, and now seems to be achieving, projects that galvanize the country's energies and allow its regions to develop and prosper without the crushing tutelage of Buenos Aires.

5

Patagonia

It was several years before we visited Patagonia but once we had 'discovered' it, the South became irresistible. When our boys were old enough to go tramping and camping, they headed south to the Andes and the Atlantic Coast, right to Tierra del Fuego. That was in the sixties and it was a time of trial for parents whose authority and 'qualifications' were being challenged the world over as never before, though I think the situation in Argentina was less virulent than in the Northern Hemisphere. When the boys went off staggering under huge rucksacks, quite well equipped with everything except money, we had to try to show enthusiasm for these positive steps towards growing up and facing life. In reality, it was difficult to imagine the region they were visiting - mountains, forests, rivers, snow and ice, wild animals maybe - it was *terra incognita* to us.

One of these trips started out as a week at the seaside, Villa Gesell in fact, but the opportunities to go further and further south arose and could not be rejected. Our first clue to this extended wanderlust was a postcard from the last town in continental Argentina. It was also the last postcard because after that there was never enough money even for a stamp.

But that journey in the vast, unpopulated south, had been tough, the boys had learned what it meant to be hungry, cold, tired and penniless. They had loaded sacks of potatoes on to a ship in Ushuaia harbour to earn something to keep going, they had sheltered in fire-stations, isolated missions and sheep ranches, and finally they were allowed to accompany a truck driver bound for Buenos Aires on condition they mended the tyres for him as necessary. These were in such dreadful condition, it was a wonder the truck ever reached its destination. When the boys finally appeared, thinner, taller, filthy and hungry, they weren't really boys any more, they were almost adults.

Geographically, Patagonia consists of the southern provinces of Neuquén, Río Negro, Chubut, Santa Cruz and Tierra del Fuego. Its seemingly boundless expanses were, until about 1880, the domain of the Araucanian Indians, more often referred to today as Mapuches. Continental Patagonia had never been systematically occupied by the European conquerors of South America, though there had been some sporadic attempts at establishing settlements along the Atlantic coast. A few adventurers had visited the shores and Jesuit missionaries had crossed the Andes from Chile but, in general, it was considered inhospitable, hostile and devoid of riches. It was Patagonia - *tierra maldita*, an accursed land, as Darwin is reported to have said. Yet just

Author in Tierra del Fuego

Patagonia

before his death he confessed that it was the memory of Patagonia which was constantly before him and which caused him the greatest emotion.

Magellan was the first European to land on the coast, staying some months in San Julian Bay in 1520 on his voyage round the globe. He named the inhabitants Patagones, after the dog-headed monster Patagon in the sixteenth century romance *Amadís de Gaula*, on account of their thick hair, heavy fur clothing and painted faces. The first Jesuits came in 1617 from what is now Chile and by the beginning of the eighteenth century, mostly as a result of their reports and writings, there was a general idea of what Patagonia represented. The Spanish rulers began to consider it prudent to make more diligent studies of the immense territory, in order to consolidate their dominion and a series of surveys and trial settlements was ordered.

The original inhabitants of present-day Argentina south of latitude 34°S belonged to various peaceful tribes: Querandís, Pampas, Puelches, Patagones and Pehuenches. Some Mapuches from Chile appeared in the area in 1700 as pressure by the Spanish invaders on their own territory on the other side of the Andes became stronger. They were an eminently warlike race, the first to confront the Spaniards valiantly with a resistance of heroic dimensions and which was to last until the final decades of the nineteenth century on both sides of the Andes. They are described in the great sixteenth-century poem 'La Araucana, the Epic of Chile' written by Alonso de Ercilla y Zuñiga and which can be appreciated in an inspired English translation by the late Walter Owen of Buenos Aires, published in Argentina in 1945. Owen renders Ercilla's description of the Araucanians as follows:

> 'Robust and strong, hairless of lip and chin,
> Well-grown and tall above the run of men,
> Of ample shoulders and capacious chest,
> And brawny limbs thick-set with stubborn thews,
> Ready and nimble and bright-spirited,
> Haughty and daring, reckless in assault,
> Hardy and tireless, bearing undismayed
> Cold, hunger, heat and all extremities.'

Where The Devil Lost His Poncho

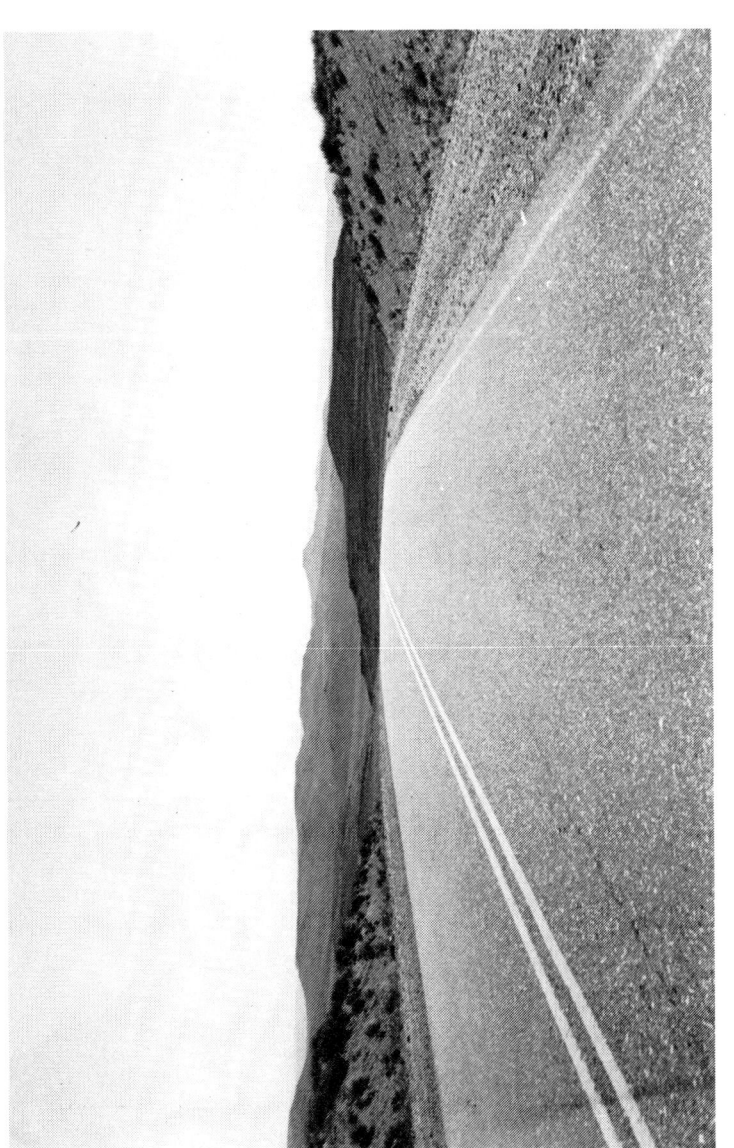

The Patagonian steppes

From the Spaniards they had learned the use of the horse and the care of cattle and sheep. As they spread over the pampa, with its fertile plains and great herds of wild cattle, they were able to dominate the indolent, pacific tribes of the region.

In 1835 one of the Mapuche Chieftains, Calfucurá, crossed the Andes from Chile with a group of 200 lancers and in a bloody, treacherous encounter with a chieftain of the plains, set himself up as the Great Chief, ruling over an area of a million square kilometres, and declaring war on the white man. He sent his emissaries to the different tribes to say that he had been chosen by the Almighty to unite all his brethren and that he would protect them from the invader. He became enormously powerful and showed great talent as ruler, leader and diplomat. With the unification of the tribes, he began the formidable dynasty of the Piedras, or Rocks, which is the meaning of the Araucanian word *curá*, his own name Calfucurá signifying Blue Rock. He was succeeded by his son who eventually came to terms with the Argentine government, while his grandson, Ceferino Namuncurá was the last 'prince' of the tribe. In Ceferino the story of his valiant race came to a radiant culmination of sanctity, the beauty of a sunset sky at the end of a stormy day.

One indication of the power of Calfucurá is the alliance he made with the governor of the Buenos Aires province, Juan Manuel Rosas, even sending him some squadrons in 1852 to help in a struggle between Rosas and General Urquiza during a period of fierce confrontation between rival political forces.

Rosas was defeated and Urquiza invited Calfucurá to negotiations in the city of Paraná. He accepted and sent an embassy, headed by his son Namuncurá. While in Paraná, Namuncurá was baptized taking the name Manuel, with Urquiza as his sponsor. All the members of his delegation were given military rank and he returned to Patagonia as Colonel Manuel Namuncurá, having signed a peace treaty with the government, by which he promised to bring to an end the ferocious Indian raids on the white settlements in exchange for recognition of Indian rights to land.

There were grave, compelling reasons for recognizing Indian power and dealing with their representative as equals. A terrible menace of desolation and death hung daily over the white population that was slowly pushing south and west to develop farms, ranches and townships in the hinterland of Buenos Aires. After the signing of the treaty, however, the Indian attacks in fact intensified as simultaneously the government did little to honour its own part of the treaty, until in 1872 Calfucurá was heavily defeated in a pitched battle and the following year he died.

Manuel Namuncurá was 62 when he succeeded as Chief and proved equally astute and skilful as his father, 'a true chip off the old stony block' according to Diego Newberry in his book, *Pampa Grass*, the biography of his father Jorge Newberry, published in English in Buenos Aires, 1953. He made a proposal to the Argentine government offering peace in exchange for assistance and provisions through the mediation of the Salesian missionary Monsignor Federico Añeiros. Nevertheless, the encroachment upon Indian territory continued, with the government making new fortifications and sending more troops to man the 'frontier'. A recommendation to form a series of towns and settle people there instead of constructing forts and filling them with soldiers was rejected and the following year saw great waves of Indian lancers descending over a front of 1,500 kilometres, leaving many dead among the burning farms and towns, and carrying away hundreds of women and children, and thousands of cattle, horses and sheep.

With the advent of a new war minister, General Julio A. Roca, the government decided to settle the Indian question once and for all with the utmost vigour. Before beginning operations in 1878, Roca offered peace to Namuncurá. Diego Newberry, in *Pampa Grass*, refers to this as 'rock meets rock', since *roca* is the Spanish word for rock, a strange coincidence in Patagonian history. Namuncurá would be given the choice of land where he and his Mapuche families could live and work, he would receive a salary and military rank would be extended to some of his captains. Namuncurá refused, he preferred to die, true to the tradition of his race, rather than submit.

The Desert Expeditionary Army of Roca, however, crushed his forces thoroughly and mercilessly, although it required three years to do so. At the end of 1882, when Namuncurá was 72 years old and driven into the fastnesses of the Andean valleys, a task force discovered his refuge and took all his family prisoner although he himself escaped. The following year he gave himself up in the hope of obtaining clemency for his beaten race. Little did this avail and the government abandoned the Indians to the degradation that has been the tragic lot of the original inhabitants of the Americas.

It seems that only now is it dawning on the Western conscience that the dispossession and near-extermination of the natives of both North and South America were criminal in the extreme. In the case of South America, however, the persistence of the so-called 'Black Legend' fomented by the Anglo-Saxons against the Spanish conquest has greatly exaggerated annihilation of the Indians.

It is easily observable that among the peoples of Latin America Indian blood is overwhelmingly predominant, with the exception of Argentina and Uruguay where the original populations never reached important numbers. This brings to mind the sarcastic comment that the Mexicans descended from the Aztecs, the Peruvians descended from the Incas, the Colombians from the Mayas, while the Argentines descended from the boats.

If the alleged genocides had in fact occurred, the Indian features of the present-day inhabitants would be scarce indeed, as is the case of North America. In addition, the word genocide implies a deliberate policy of elimination and there is no valid basis for such accusations. European diseases introduced by the invaders probably accounted for enormous numbers of deaths.

As far as Patagonia is concerned, the Indians were hounded out of their ancestral territories which were awarded to high-ranking officers of the Desert Army and eventually to powerful foreign firms or plain immigrants, with a generosity matched only by the harshness of the treatment given to the native races. Of course, the 'discovery' and seizure of lands were not confined to the Americas. Africa, the Pacific Islands, including Australia and New Zealand, the Indian sub continent and other parts of Asia were all fair game for the insatiable greed and overbearing conceit of the dominating Europeans. Now in pronounced decline, the white man is witnessing the stirring of a new awareness of identity among the once-despised 'lesser breeds'.

One redeeming feature in the story of the white man in Patagonia is the work of the Salesians, the Order of St. Francis de Sales. Their work in the Patagonian outposts began in 1879 and has been heroic and prolific. Father Milanesio, for instance, who baptized Ceferino, worked there for thirty-four years during which time he crossed the Andes on horseback twenty-seven times and from 1886 to 1914 rode more than 65,000 kilometres, covering 7,200 in a single year. He is but one of the many Salesians who rode immense distances to bring the Faith, education, medicine and protection to the defeated Araucanians and the struggling settlers.

Perhaps the most outstanding of all was Giovanni Cagliero, known as the 'Foreman of Patagonia', who eventually became a Cardinal and died in Rome in 1926. He had lived among the tribe of Namuncurá and had crossed over to Chile to erect colleges and churches there as well. Cagliero's spiritual and material work has flourished greatly and continues to be everywhere apparent in the constant Salesian activity in Patagonia.

However, Patagonia is still today a dilated, thinly-populated territory already exploited for the extraction of its natural resources to benefit principally the macrocephalous metropolitan area. The average Argentine has, not surprisingly, shown little enthusiasm for facing the rigours of life in the region, especially since other parts of Argentina enjoy a benign climate, fertile land and access to modern amenities. A few flourishing areas do attract settlers, like the River Negro valley devoted to fruit-farming and related industries, the oilfields of Neuquén, Chubut and Santa Cruz, the River Chubut basin with its agricultural economy pioneered by Welsh immigrants who arrived in the 1890s, the tourist areas on the Atlantic beaches and in the Andean Lakelands, and Tierra del Fuego at 'the uttermost ends of the earth'.

The coastal waters of Patagonia are breeding grounds for the huge southern right whale (*Eubalaena australis*) and in the Southern Hemisphere winter and spring important numbers congregate in the neighbourhood of the Valdés Península, on latitude 42°S, where the calm and relatively shallow waters fringed by high cliff and rock formations give optimum conditions for these thirty-ton monsters and their babies.

The whales devote much of their time to leaping from the water, making a half-roll in the air and crashing back into the sea. It is

Patagonia

suggested that these acrobatics may have a purpose of communication between the members of the group and could also help them eliminate external parasites and pieces of superficial skin. Another 'trick' observed is when the whales stand on their heads with the great tail fin protruding from the sea like a sail, the wind blowing it along in an outsize version of wind-surf.

The whales have only one serious predator (apart from humans) and that is the orca, otherwise they maintain a close relationship with other species such as dolphins, seals and sea elephants. The Valdés Península is, in fact, a headquarters of the sea elephant and is the only continental breeding place in the world, as in all other cases they occupy island territories. An observation platform has been built at a prudent distance on the clifftops, so that the many tourists can observe the creatures without provoking unsuitable or dangerous conditions and to avoid the possibility that the animals might abandon the area if they were interfered with too much by unthinking, over-curious visitors.

Year after year the Patagonian coasts are visited by enormous contingents of penguins which colonize land near the sea in order to nest and raise their chicks. They share this habitat with numerous other species of sea birds and they are relatively safe from predators. Some years ago, a foreign company offered to install a factory to process the penguins and export their meat and oil. Fortunately the local reaction was a horrified NO, unimpressed by the vast profits reportedly involved. Obviously, no creature is safe from human rapacity.

Other gregarious birds are the flamingos which make their strange nests in lake-edge colonies that can number 25,000 birds. The nests, made of mud, are constructed by the male, using his trowel-shaped beak for the purpose and they take the form of a levelled-off cone with a depression in the middle for the eggs. From 10 days of age until the young flamingos can fly at about 3 months, they are kept together in 'crèches' comprising several thousand juveniles under the vigilance of a few adults.

Another inhabitant of Patagonia is the Argentine variety of ostrich, the Ñandú, which belongs to the group of primitive birds such as kiwis and emus. It is extremely rapid, has acute vision and an insatiable appetite. Fights between the males are often ferocious, with necks entwined to choking point and powerful legs kicking murderously. Some Indian tribes see a Ñandú pursued by dogs and hunters in the Southern Cross and others identify it in the Pleiades constellation. A legend explains its habit of hiding its head in the sand, according to which the Ñandú used to visit Heaven but because of its dissipated customs, God told it to get out and not return until further notice. When it insisted it should be let back in, the door slammed against its head. Thus, whenever it gets a fright, the first thing it does is to hide its head, remembering that painful experience.

Patagonia was always a land of mystery, legends and myths, where anything was possible, the land of the absurd, the bizarre and the picturesque. Since the days of the Conquest it attracted legions of treasure-seekers who, on the whole, fared very badly and found little conventional treasure.

In 1528 Francisco Cesar returned to his base in what is now Paraguay, from an expedition across the pampa to the foothills of the Andes. During this journey he heard of a fabulous city, a sort of urban Eden, of gold, silver and precious stones in everyday use, as well as fountains of eternal youth. Whoever entered the city, however, could never leave it. This was the southern counterpart of the fabled El Dorado in the northern New World and became known as the City of the Cesars, named after the first expeditionaries, Francisco Cesar and his brothers. Countless attempts were made to find the City, in spite of the continuous failure of all expeditions, even those which were most imposing and well-equipped.

The Magic City was the most persistent of the legends that included monsters and giants in the Patagonian habitat but there has been no scarcity of audacious adventurers and dreamers. A French citizen, Orllie-Antoine de Tounens, of Peregueaux, appeared in Coquimbo, Chile, in August 1858, having contacted the tribes on both sides of the Andes with presents and demonstrations of goodwill and proposing to the Mapuche Chieftain Quilapán liberation from Argentina and Chile. Finally in November 1869, with the prestige of Quilapán firmly behind him, he declared himself a monarch:

'We, Prince Orllie-Antoine de Tounens, considering that Araucania does not belong to any other state, that it is divided into tribes and that a central government is required, both in the individual and the general interest,
Decree herewith:
Article 1: A constitutional hereditary monarchy is founded in Araucania and prince Orllie-Antoine de Tounens is named King . . .'!

At the same time he sent a message to the President of Chile announcing the creation of an independent, Araucanian state. With the evidence of support from many other Patagonian tribes he proclaimed that Patagonia was now integrated into his Kingdom and thus 'Orllie-Antoine I, by the Grace of God King of Araucania', had created an empire of almost two million square kilometres, all in the space of ninety-six hours. As Manuel Porcel de Peralta observes in his *Bibliografía del Nahuel Huapi*, 'Not even Napoleon did anything so prodigious.'

The following year he fell into a trap laid for him by the Chilean authorities and was brought to trial in Santiago. He narrowly missed execution and was finally deported to France in 1862 after the French Ambassador in Santiago convinced the judge that obviously Orllie-Antoine was not sane. Sane or otherwise, he reappeared in Argentina in 1868 and once again contacted the Mapuches in Patagonia promising them modern arms which would be brought to the Chilean port of Valdivia in a French warship.

The consequent ferment in the tribes alerted the Chileans who took severe measures to put an end to this new attempt and set a considerable price on the head of the French liberator of the Indians. Forewarned by his loyal 'Private Secretary', an adventurous young Italian who had accompanied him on his return to his Kingdom, Orllie-Antoine managed to escape to Buenos Aires, where he failed to raise the slightest interest in his cause. He returned to France and died in 1878 in his native city being 'succeeded by his heir Gustave Archilles I'. Apparently the 'Court of Araucania' still exists, recognized only by itself, and claims the throne of Araucania to this day.

The story of Orllie-Antoine brings to mind the equally curious history of Julius Popper. He was born in Bucharest in 1857 and at the age of 16 or 17 he left home and made for Paris where he studied engineering. After journeying to Japan, China and India, he appeared in New Orleans where he carried out some engineering work only to move on to Cuba, Mexico and Brazil. In Brazil he heard of the discovery of gold in the far south of Argentina so he immediately sailed for Buenos Aires.

The story was that the ship *Villarino* had been grounded in 1884 near Cape Vírgenes and while the crew waited for a rescue expedition to come from Punta Arenas in southern Chile, they found gold deposited on the beaches by the furious waves of the Magellan Straits.

Popper joined the gold seekers but he did it in style. He formed a Company and went to Cape Vírgenes to see for himself. What he saw convinced him that prospects would be much better on the neighbouring island of Tierra del Fuego, where he obtained mining concessions and set up various establishments, the most important being El Páramo. In 1881 he had about seventy employees, mostly Yugoslavs, working for him on the wild, desolate shores of the island. Writing of these unusual goldmines, Popper reports:

'Like the Jupiter of mythology, the king of metals makes his appearance on the Fuegian shores in the midst of thunderous, fearful noise.

'The sovereign Gold needs the roar of the furious elements, of storms unleashed, in order to make his brilliant entry on the stage . . .

'When the fury of the elements dies down, the dark sky lightens and the waters recede, the area has a completely different appearance. Whatever had been on the beach before has disappeared, new belts of black sands can be seen piled up here and there, according to the whim of the waves that originated them, and on examining these sands particles of gold, more or less abundant, from the size of a grain of corn to an imperceptible, microscopic flake, are to be found gleaming among the magnetic iron of which the sands are made.'

Popper soon became a legendary figure. He was said to have his own army and to have made his own coins and postage stamps. Serious research into his life and activities in Tierra del Fuego does not fully support the speculations about 'Popper's Empire' or his 'Army'. He certainly saw himself in the rôle of a 'Civilizer of barbarians' the customary attitude of the contemporary white man in all walks of life.

Popper referred harshly and disdainfully to the local Ona Indians and photographs circulated showing him apparently involved in a slaying of aborigines in 1887 in Tierra del Fuego. It is always possible, however, that he was made the scapegoat for all those who regarded progress almost as an article of faith.

In 1891 he seemed to have moderated his opinions. He had begun to understand the devastating effect of the encounter between the white civilization and the 'backward' Onas; between the invaders only interested in exploiting the land and the nomadic tribes for whom the habitat belonged in common to all and provided them with the essentials of life.

As evidence of his change of heart, and two years before his untimely death in 1893, he drew up for presentation to the Argentine government a detailed plan for colonizing and civilizing the Indians. Along with his other characteristically ground-breaking initiatives, the project failed to interest the faraway bureaucrats of Buenos Aires. It is probable that if Popper had lived he would have insisted energetically on the merits of his proposals.

Popper was a lively mixture of scientist, explorer, inventor, businessman, engineer and writer who moved with natural ease among the élite of Buenos Aires. Perhaps his eccentricities led to the many rumours about his ultimate intentions but the truth is that he served Argentina very well and generously at a crucial time in its history. This was when Chile was challenging Argentina for every inch of the southern lands. Popper claimed he had extracted more than half a ton of gold in the few years he ran his mining establishments and, more important in the long run, he had explored and mapped much of Tierra del Fuego, naming mountains, rivers and lakes and reporting the results of his activities to the Argentine geographical and scientific societies.

His activities ended abruptly with his sudden death in Buenos

Aires from a heart attack at the age of 37 in 1893, to the great consternation of his many friends and acquaintances. Legends about him persist to this day, maybe because they are the kind of myth that Patagonia has always inspired in the imagination.

Patagonia witnessed also the escapades of Butch Cassidy who had had a notorious criminal career in the U.S. and had sailed to Argentina in 1901 when the authorities were closing in on him. He started a ranch in the province of Chubut, accompanied by the Sundance Kid and his companion Etta Place. By 1905 the ranch was flourishing but apparently the old habits proved too strong and the members of the gang returned to their misdeeds with a series of assaults on banks. Finally, they disappeared into the Andes with the police hot on their heels and nothing certain is known of their further adventures and eventual deaths.

Martin Sheffield was another American who attained fame in Patagonia in the early years of this century. He was a Texan cowboy who had come to work for some English ranchers in the neighbourhood of Bariloche after unspecified gold-digging activities in the Andes. An attractive, picturesque figure, he had a great reputation as a marksman and his capacity to down gin was legendary. One day in 1930 he created an enormous sensation by announcing that he had discovered near Lake Epuyen the tracks of a huge monster, a kind of gigantic lizard. It was assumed to be a dinosaur and the impact caused was reflected in scientific circles and newspapers of the whole world.

The director of the Buenos Aires Zoo, Clemente Onelli, was pressured into organizing a scientific expedition to 'bring it back alive' in the prevailing conviction that anything was possible in Patagonia. The area of the monster's appearance was thoroughly explored without finding any more tracks and the expedition had to admit shamefacedly that Mr Sheffield's monster could only be the result of a large overdose of gin.

A more specific monster exists in the local lore of the region though it has proved as elusive as its Loch Ness counterpart as far as definite proof is concerned. The Indians are convinced of its existence and they carefully train their children to avoid walking in the shallow water at the lakeshores. It is known as 'El Cuero' which means animal hide, and has the shape of an open cowskin. To cross the water it rolls itself into the form of a long, thick tree-trunk and then floats unrolled into a strategic position in the shallows to await its prey. It is the colour of the earth although it can also be green or black. Stretched out in the low water, the lapping waves gradually cover it with sand so that it becomes difficult to see. The person or animal that is unlucky enough to tread on it feels overcome by dizziness and then the Cuero suddenly lifts up its sides, showing many sharp claws or hooks with which it imprisons its victim, whereupon it descends to the bottom of the lake to enjoy its meal.

There are stories of other lake-dwelling monsters, one known as the 'Bien Peinado' or 'well-combed one'. The name refers to the long hair or mane which looks sleekly combed when the creature rears its head out of the water. Otherwise descriptions are vague.

Reports began just a few years ago about the sighting of a large monster in Lake Nahuel Huapi, in the vicinity of Bariloche, but it is considered suspect as its appearances coincide with the height of the tourist season. The local press has given it the nickname 'Nahuelito', which is the diminutive of Nahuel, perhaps as an analogy of the pet name Nessie for its Loch Ness relative.

Legends about Patagonia include references to the springs of eternal life and indeed there are many thermal springs all along the Andes, often in inaccessible places. A well-known, accessible example is Mount Copahue (pronounced Co-pa-way). It could be Argentina's Magic Mountain though of course it is quite unlike the Zauberberg of Thomas Mann. Instead, it is a snow-covered, dormant volcano rising nearly 9,000 feet in the heart of the Andes in the mountain province of Neuquén, where it pours out a variety of health-restoring water and mud in the beautiful, desolate landscape of the region.

In the language of the Mapuche inhabitants, Copahue means 'place of sulphur', from *copa* – sulphur, and *hue* – place. According to the geologists the volcano appears to be using its last cartridges, contenting itself with throwing up some gases and ash now and then. Thousands of years ago it stopped spewing out lava and rocks and its heat is now not sufficient to melt the icefields on its slopes.

The hot springs are located in a glacier-excavated depression at

6,000 feet above sea level and although the facilities may seem unpretentious to visitors who are acquainted with the elegant spas of Europe and elsewhere, they are adequate and constantly being improved. The resort is within the reach of a wide sector of the population, as the cost of treatment is reasonable and access to it is no longer so difficult. The 100-mile road to Copahue from the railhead is now paved, running through rugged mountain terrain and splendid scenery, alternating between fertile, wooded valleys and high, rolling moors in a context of impressive geological upheaval.

The region is sparsely populated, the few lonely villages or very small towns along the way struggling to survive in a mostly inhospitable environment and physical isolation. It is, of course, possible to reach Copahue by air as there is a direct plane service from Neuquén City, the capital of the province, a mere forty minutes away as the condor flies.

Ten miles south of Copahue lies Lake Caviahue (*cavia* - bitter, and *hue* - place) formed by the river Agrio which rises in the volcano.

Volcano Copahue

Agrio is the Spanish word for bitter and the river is indeed bitter to taste, while the lake itself is without game fish for that very reason. Numerous waterfowl including black-necked swans, however, seem happy enough with the situation. Eventually, the river loses its acidity as it goes on its course and is fed by innumerable streams of fresh water.

The river flows out from the crater of the volcano which holds a lagoon of clear water bordered by a glacier. Water taken directly from the crater is said to have a fulminating effect on anyone unwise enough to drink it although, conversely, two drops a day increasing by one drop to a maximum of fifteen and then decreasing back to two drops is claimed to be a definite cure for digestive troubles. A flow of light grey mud also spills over the lip of the crater and is piped into the spa area and down to the hotel on the shores of Lake Caviahue. The village of Caviahue, which has some permanent residents, is very new dating back only to 1985, so new, in fact, that it has no cemetery.

In Caviahue the beauty of the Andean scene is enhanced by the presence of large numbers of araucanian pines, which are practically the only variety of tree in the area and they belong to the family of conifers found only in the Southern Hemisphere. It has sharply-pointed, overlapping, triangular leaves arranged spirally on stiff branches, providing the tree with formidable protection against animals in general.

The araucaria is known elsewhere as monkey puzzle but it is unlikely that monkeys would be found in the high Andean habitat of this tree. It can rise to a height of 150 feet and its trunk can reach a diameter of five feet, and fine stands of this living fossil still flourish, although in a comparatively reduced area on both sides of the Andes. The large cones or fruit of the araucaria are composed of tightly-packed clove-like seeds, rich in proteins, and they were the basic food of local tribes. They are still appreciated for their nutritional value.

The araucarias mark the tree line, since not far above Caviahue they, too, disappear. This ancient plant seems highly appropriate in conjunction with the shattered, moonscape approaches to the volcano and the numerous hissing fumeroles and bubbling sulphurous pools.

It is possible to ride up to the top of the volcano on horseback, an apparently popular excursion, though not for the faint-hearted. Moreover, for those fanatics who want to go right to the 'source', the guides will lower them five metres over the edge of the crater with ropes, into the lukewarm waters of the lagoon. The greatest danger is the possibility of catching pneumonia on being hauled out of the water and into the below-zero temperature of the mountain. For the most part, the visitors to Copahue have come seeking relief from a host of infirmities: arthritis, coxalgia or hip-joint disease, rheumatism, sciatica, psoriasis, acne, neurodermitis, seborrhoea and other skin complaints, chronic bronchitis, sinusitis, respiratory ailments and so on. There have even been positive results in the treatment of hemiplegia and cerebral paralysis.

Activity in Copahue is restricted to the Southern Hemisphere summer period from December to mid-April. By April there are the first signs of the long winter which will cover the entire place with up to eight metres of snow and only in November will it become accessible again. Then it will be necessary to repair, paint and build to be ready for the visitors, to start new construction and to advance as far as possible before the next winter. Upkeep of the resort is a constant struggle against the elements, the corrosive nature of the minerals and the vapours themselves and, in particular, against the severity of the winter.

Upon arrival patients first visit the medical centre where they undergo a compulsory revue of their state of health, and it is recommended that to be really effective, treatment should involve fifteen to twenty days' stay. The abundant varieties of mineral and medicinal waters are applied, on the one hand, for general therapeutic action: de-sensitization, detoxication, as a sedative or for diaphoretic and diuretic action. On the other hand, the waters are used for local topical action: hydrothermal therapy and application of mud or mud mixed with algae.

Indoor facilities are housed in simple, strong constructions around the edge of the lagoons and include immersion baths, steam rooms and small cubicles for resting after each treatment. The immersion baths are installed in individual rooms and consist of large, wooden tubs, filled directly from the lagoons with either sulphurous, sulphated or ferruginous waters, their temperature being adjusted as necessary with cold water. As regards the steam baths, for example for cases of sinusitis, it does not require much imagination to think they might be ante-rooms of Dante's Inferno. Beneath the open floorboards, the sulphurous spring seethes noisily and the room is filled with clouds of steam. The patient is shut in like a lost soul but, mercifully, the number of minutes inside is carefully controlled by the attendants.

The different kinds of mud, classified as sulphurous, sulphated ferrous, aluminous and magnesian silicated, have varying temperatures, strength and colours and each kind has its specific healing qualities. Naturally, the beneficial effects of the waters are complemented by the high-mountain climate which is, on the whole, very agreeable in summer and autumn, with the clearest of skies and warm sunshine, although there are frequent sharp drops in temperature and even flurries of snow.

Open-air installations comprise the lagoons known as 'Del Chancho' (of the Pig) and 'Verde' (Green). The Laguna del Chancho is tepid enough to wallow in contentedly, although it is alongside another large pool which appears to be boiling furiously and belches great clouds of steam into the cool air. Local folklore includes some lurid descriptions of what happens to anyone who has the misfortune to fall into this angry cauldron.

The Laguna Verde is pleasantly warm and bubbles continuously providing, on bright sunny days one of the favourite spots for visitors to congregate and yarn about their ailments and cures. There are also many permanent springs of drinking water, named according to their special thermal characteristics and properties: Vichy, Sulphur, Lemon and Maté, this last one hot enough to brew your tea or *maté*.

Close to Copahue itself, there are some other thermal bath facilities called 'Las Máquinas' while yet another is a do-it-yourself location known as 'Las Maquinitas'. Here the steam comes hissing noisily out of the mountainside, the sound being reminiscent of an engine room and is presumably the reason for the name. Among the rocks, people have made little pools of warm, muddy water in which they dangle their feet and legs and plaster their painful joints with mud. Someone even managed to erect a steam bath by making a little chamber with rocks piled around a convenient fumerole.

The first recorded case of successful treatment in Copahue dates back to 1865 when the Argentine doctor Pedro Ortíz Vélez recommended that a young Chilean girl who was very ill be taken there for therapy. After twenty days' treatment she made a remarkable recovery. At that time access to the area was controlled by the Indian Chief Cheuquel, known as the Prince of the Pines and, according to local accounts, he always permitted sick people to go through his territory to Copahue.

Others who pioneered in the study of the thermal springs were Dr. Pablo Groeber who carried out geological and hydrological research and Dr. Herrero Ducloux who made complete analyses of the waters and the muds. Almost a figure of folklore was a long-time settler in the region, the guide Zambo Jara who used to take the first patients to the springs. He offered them accommodation in his own modest dwelling and had a string of horses to take the more adventurous patients right to the lagoon in the crater of the volcano.

Progress achieved in Copahue and Caviahue in the last decades owes much to a Polish immigrant, Mecislao Bialous, born in Warsaw, who came to Argentina in 1948. On a visit to Copahue he sensed its potential importance and dedicated his efforts towards its development. Now it has a capacity for 2,000 baths per day and well over 6,000 people receive treatment in Copahue during a season.

Experimental geothermal energy equipment was inaugurated on the volcano in 1988 to study the possibility of providing power to the region. At present power is brought from the hydroelectric power station at the Chocón Dam about 300 miles away, but naturally there is great interest in studying the feasibility of using the geothermal energy right at hand.

Copahue has electric light and running water, post office and radio-telephone. The Argentine Automobile Club runs a service station and there is a campsite for trailers and tents, apart from a variety of hotels. Three times a week a fair or market is held when the country people from neighbouring Chile cross over to sell typical products: ponchos, blankets, basket work, herbs, fruit and vegetables. In reality, Argentina shares its magic mountain with Chile and on the western slopes inside Chile there is also a hot springs centre, known as Chanchocó.

The whole area of Copahue and Caviahue abounds in streams and waterfalls some of which are remarkably beautiful, such as the one named the Cabellera de la Virgen (the Virgin's Tresses). Another impressive fall is the Cascada del Agrio where the river drops fifty metres from an overhanging, almost circular basalt rim into a narrow canyon.

Above the treeline the rugged vegetation gradually dwindles, leaving great expanses of shattered rocks and tumbled boulders, yet in among this arid debris there are lovely flowers - purple, yellow, white, blue. Their delightful, unexpected presence on such forbidding slopes calls to mind Thomas Gray's flower 'born to blush unseen, and waste its sweetness on the desert air'. In the autumn, the bright green ñire bush, which grows abundantly among the sombre araucarias, turns to intense yellows, russets and purples, in a final glorious overspill of colour before the onslaught of winter.

One of the approaches to Copahue descends a long way into a broad green valley crowned on both sides by towering black basalt formations, and later it winds up slowly again to break out into the open where Lake Caviahue sparkles in the distance. The valley is part of the Indian reserve and the Mapuches bring their herds up here for the summer grazing - a few cattle, innumerable small white goats and an impressive number of strikingly beautiful horses. These are of the famed criollo breed, relatively small in stature but tireless and surefooted, the same breed that Tschiffely took on his 10,000 mile ride from Buenos Aires to Washington. The herds of goats and cattle provide most of the Mapuche's needs, a few animals being sold now and then to buy extras. The only dwellings belong to the Indians and the land cannot be bought or sold.

The school follows the people to the summer grazing lands and until quite recently, it consisted of two large trailers. Most tourists passing by found it difficult to resist a visit to this lonely outpost of education, as could be seen from the Visitors' Book with its pages of signatures and affectionate messages and contributions. Few city dwellers fail to react with frank admiration and emotion at the sight of the tiny mobile school perched on a remote Andean mountainside and of its undaunted teacher.

Caviahue is destined to become a great ski centre. The Neuquén Province has constructed a well-equipped vacation complex devoted mainly to ski activities. It could become one of the world's finest sites for this sport because of the quality of the snow, the length of the season and the superlative slopes. An added advantage for ski enthusiasts from other parts of the world is, naturally, that the winter season occurs here during the Northern Hemisphere summer.

It is equipped with various types of ski-lifts, there are seven kilometres of free descent for Alpine skiing and boundless possibilities for the cross-country variety. The centre also offers the other types of winter sports which have now become popular, including huskie-drawn sledges and snowboards. Some skiers have been known to take advantage of their mid-winter visit to Copahue to have a dip in the warm, snow-free Laguna Verde, using a ladder to get down and up the high wall of snow surrounding the lagoons.

Copahue and Caviahue offer a rare combination of health and beauty, an opportunity to soak the body in their healing waters and to drench the spirit with the incomparable beauty of the high mountains.

Four hundred miles to the south lies San Carlos de Bariloche, the so-called 'Capital of the Southern Lakes'.

Its history began when in 1894, Carlos Wiederhold, a Chilean businessman of German descent trading between southern Chile and Argentina, decided to cross the Andes from Chile through the magnificent but at that time little-known Pérez Rosales Pass which leads directly to Lake Nahuel Huapi. It seems he was so impressed with this beautiful region that in February of the following year he built himself a house on a site that is now the centre of the town of San Carlos de Bariloche.

The town was officially 'born' on 3 May 1902, having 850 inhabitants at that moment. Its birth certificate was in fact a decree signed by the President of Argentina, setting aside the specific tract of land known as Colonia Agrícola San Carlos. Presumably, the bureaucracy in Buenos Aires subsequently prepared the layout of the streets of the future town, a misfortune which could never be rectified later.

The design followed the chequer-board pattern used all over the country, which is acceptable and highly practical in flat terrain, but little short of disastrous on the steep contours of mountain country

Some streets end abruptly in a long flight of stairs or directly in a retaining wall and every winter there are numerous incidents and accidents when all kinds of vehicles are unable to make the grade and descend out of control, with the results imaginable.

These streets are also hard on pedestrians who endure countless falls on the precipitous, icy sidewalks, creating a growing demand for traumatologists. The imposition of metropolitan criteria on the rest of the country, as illustrated by the Bariloche town plan, caused much resentment in the provinces over the years which, up to now as mentioned earlier, found the declared philosophy of federalism to be for the most part merely theoretical.

Bariloche took its name from the Indian Vuriloche tribe of the district: *Vuri* - beyond, *lo* - hill and *che* - people, hence, the people from the other side of the hill. It is said that San Carlos was added in honour of the patron saint of Carlos Wiederhold but Bariloche is the name now used almost exclusively.

After Wiederhold built his house, the town began to grow, mostly due to the thriving trade with the Chilean port of Puerto Montt on the Pacific and thus with Europe and other points abroad. The population forming the new town was a medley of the original Mapuches, Chileans, Germans, Austrians, Swiss, Spaniards and Italians and, here and there, an Argentine. Many of the Europeans had crossed the Andes from Chile where work for colonists was becoming increasingly hard to find.

Far from other Argentine centres of population, the nearest being 300 miles away, in the isolation imposed by the lack of communications in the first years of the twentieth century, Bariloche was a disorderly refuge for many dubious characters, as well as regular settlers trying to build up a future. The general scarcity of women was part of the Patagonian scene and is still the case in some parts today, and it led to many scandalous situations that Bariloche took in its stride as unavoidable.

Perhaps some order was achieved after 1905 when the Salesian missionary Father Milanesio established the first church, but at all events, the area began to make headway with the hard work, vision and indomitable spirit of such dynamic pioneers as Primo Capraro, Emilio Frey and Christian Boock.

By the time the railroad reached Bariloche in December 1934, the boisterous village had become a town of about 6,000 inhabitants, unlike any other Argentine town, with a charm of its own, framed in the stupendous scenery of lakes, mountains and forests. It was already at that time important as a centre serving a wide rural area with its ranches, farms and scattered settlements. A year or two before the arrival of the railroad, the organized urbanization of Bariloche and the development of the Nahuel Huapi National Park had begun.

This National Park, the first in Argentina, dates back to 1903 and had been created with the donation to the State of three square leagues (about fifteen square miles) near Bariloche, by the geographer Francisco Pascasio Moreno, who had skilfully and successfully carried out the technical and practical work of defining the Andean boundaries between Argentina and Chile. Moreno was a man of rare talent – scientist, explorer, palaeontologist – whose contributions to the prestige and integrity of his country received scant gratitude from the authorities of his time. When he died in 1919, no representative of the government attended his funeral, there was no echo in the press, many people never knew he had lived. It was monumental ingratitude but nowadays no doubt exists about his place as one of Argentina's finest citizens.

Now in 1937 came the team of planners headed by an outstanding architect Ezequiel Bustillo and the inhabitants of Bariloche saw with astonishment how the town was transformed. The architecture, in stone and timber, followed a style previously unknown in Argentina and was unkindly and probably unjustly referred to as 'pseudo-Bavarian'. Construction began of the Civil Center or Town Square, the hospital, schools, hotels large and small, including the majestic Hotel Llao-Llao, the Cathedral and two small chapels in Llao-Llao and on Mount Catedral, the Patagonian Museum, a salmon and trout rearing station, the National Park headquarters and a dock on the lakeside. In fact Bariloche was to become a centre for international tourism and, as suggested by Manuel Porcel de Peralta in his book, *Biografia del Nahuel Huapi*, already referred to, the legendary City of the Cesars sought for during so many centuries finally materialized.

Before the railroad came, Bariloche was reached only by difficult dirt roads across the Patagonian wilderness. Tourists from Buenos

Aires and points north could travel by rail to Neuquen some 300 miles to the north and then continue in the large motor cars of a transport company created in 1912, forerunner of the overland buses. The intrepid passengers included an ex-president of the U.S., Theodore Roosevelt, who reportedly had some fine fishing in the Bariloche lake district.

It was the end of the 1960s before the roads were finally paved all the way to Bariloche and also before there were air-conditioned, dust-proof trains on the route, to soften the rigours of the journey. After that, the little Andean town with timber houses and steep shingled roofs was engulfed in an orgy of 'development'.

Architectural harmony and environmental appropriateness were the first victims as the urban blight spread alarmingly along the twenty miles of lakeside towards the dramatically beautiful locality of Llao-Llao. All this was in the name of tourism and was first checked by the ruinous state of the Argentine economy in the early 1970s. It is perhaps not ethical to rejoice over economic depressions or recessions but the drop in visitors to Bariloche was striking and by the time some recovery occurred towards the end of the decade, a series of zoning and construction regulations to control the future growth of the city had miraculously been put into effect.

I say miraculously because the regulations placed severe curbs on the activities of very powerful interest groups which are only concerned with immediate profits and move off to pastures new when the results of their 'developments' are a once-lovely landscape devoid of all enchantment. Not surprisingly, it has often proved possible to find suitable loopholes or to obtain approval for exceptions to the regulations. Yet in the long run, it is up to the citizens themselves to be vigilant, to care for their city and to participate in community affairs.

The tourist industry is, in my opinion, a very doubtful benefit to mankind, at least the way it is handled at the present time. It is true that people want to travel and are curious to see the world. However, the tendency to herd travellers along in large, depredatory contingents on one exhausting visit after another is very profitable for the organizers but little short of disastrous for the most attractive and interesting places throughout the world.

On the whole, tourism in Argentina is still a rather half-baked affair. Dare I say, Thank Goodness?

In the past when our family vacations found us exploring Argentina (as tourists, of course) it seemed that there was a conspiracy of silence to protect some especially nice places from tourist hordes. Some of our best holiday memories are of discoveries made because of a chance remark, or a wrong turning, rarely because of a poster or a tourist agent's brochure. One such example was a magnificent waterfall tumbling through a thickly wooded gorge. There were no billboards or picture postcards, only a small sign pointing to a footpath and a discreet cabin for the sale of refreshments. We had heard of it the day before in conversation with a summer resident of Bariloche.

San Carlos de Bariloche is unique in another way as it can boast the highest concentration of scientific and research activity in the whole country.

The first scientist to select Bariloche as the ideal site for serious investigation was none other than the legendary Ronald Richter, an Austrian physicist who convinced President Perón in 1946 that he could lead Argentina into the Atomic Age and provide the country with abundant, inexpensive energy for its development and industrialization. He had begun his Argentine career in Córdoba but on learning about the lake country and visiting Bariloche in 1947 he decided it was just the place for working and studying, free from the distracting sounds and pressures of the large cities, and of course from meddling bureaucrats.

Eventually, the Atomic Energy Commission took shape and its research centre was set up in Bariloche. Foreign obsession with nuclear weaponry had made Argentina suspect of warlike intentions when all the evidence seems to prove that she was not interested in anything but the peaceful application of atomic energy. Be that as it may, the story of Richter's activities in Argentina is a fascinating puzzle which nevertheless led to serious international-level research and impressive results in the field. Dr. Mario Mariscotti of the Atomic Energy Commission has told the inside story of this venture in his lively book, *The Atomic Secret of Huemul Island*, published in 1985.

Patagonia

The work of the Bariloche Atomic Center, which is only a part of a large national nuclear organization, is highly important, with the experimental reactor and the Balseiro Institute which trains top-level students for doctoral degrees in Nuclear Physics and Engineering. Connected with the work of the Center are some applied research companies, primarily concerned with developing local technology and the production of nuclear equipment of all kinds, including enriched uranium, nuclear medical equipment, electronics and computers.

In due course, other institutions were installed in Bariloche: the Agricultural and Livestock Experimental Station (INTA) which, among many other activities, carried out invaluable work to help the isolated, subsistence-level sheep and goat rearers in the bleak plateaux north and east of Bariloche; the regional branch of the University of Comahue that serves North Patagonia; and the Fundación Bariloche, a private 'think-tank' of postgraduate research and teaching.

This Bariloche Foundation is well known internationally in scientific circles, in spite of its short, chequered history. It was created in 1963 by a group of Argentine scientists and businessmen to further original, postgraduate research and the transfer of knowledge to the community as a whole. For Argentina it was a novelty and its location in Bariloche, far from the centres of activity and power, was an even greater novelty. Principle among its avowed objectives was the study of Patagonia and the needs of its inhabitants, so long regarded only as material for exploitation by the over-centralized, Buenos Aires-based political system.

In the remarkably short period of ten years, the Fundación developed its departments of Biology, Natural Resources and Energy, including Ecology and Geology, of Mathematics, a Computer Centre, Social Sciences and Music of which the famed Camerata Bariloche was its most notable creation.

In 1973 the elected Peronist government viewed the Foundation with a jaundiced eye and the more extreme sectors of the party wanted to close it down as being a tool of Yankee Imperialism. Then the military dictatorship which erupted on the scene in 1976 considered the Foundation to be a hotbed of communism and cut off all support expecting it to wither away as a result, apart from physically persecuting a few of its members.

Inevitably, the Institution had to close down most of its activities, leaving only a minimum, low-profile nucleus to try to survive. The profile was in fact so low that even the townspeople of Bariloche thought the Foundation had disappeared. It was as if it had joined the list of species in danger of extinction on which its Ecology Department had worked so strenuously. However, it survived the eight years of dictatorship and seems to have successfully endured the painful process of revival.

For Argentines as a whole, many of whom only knew Bariloche by hearsay until the mid-eighties, it was considered a veritable Paradise, a favourite place for honeymoons and for the high-school graduates' year-end trip, a land of chocolate and roses, of woollen pullovers with bold intricate designs, of skiing and trout fishing. Many Argentines had probably never seen snow falling and the Bariloche winter scene exerted on them an irresistible magnetism. They also knew that life was quite informal, that clothing could be conventional or unconventional according to mood.

Many young people attempted to settle in the area and make a new, exciting future. But Bariloche is a hard-hearted town and exacts a heavy price in one way or another for the privilege of living there. The truth is that all Patagonia is hard on the newcomer and, here again, I write from experience.

It is asserted that all newcomers have to pay, figuratively speaking, *derecho de piso*, or right of access. While Bariloche enjoys many comforts and conveniences of a modern city that are absent in much of the region, a pioneering spirit, survival ability, courage and abundance of good luck similar to those needed in the days of the early settlers, are necessary to keep body and soul together in the first few years.

There is another side to Bariloche. It is a living object lesson in how not to develop. It was unable to absorb successfully the enormous influx of new inhabitants in the seventies, which soon overwhelmed its infrastructure and services. The old-timers resented the new arrivals and both seemed unable to work together to channel the city's growth into harmonious urbanization, in order to protect its most important resource – the beauty of its surroundings. Other small, attractive towns in the mountain region, like San Martín de los Andes and El Bolsón, which are also favourite tourist attractions, claim to be determined to avoid the deterioration caused by badly-managed tourism and the resulting loss of reputation. Shakespeare, of course, has some appropriate lines about such a situation:

> '... who steals my purse steals trash;
> ... but he that filches from me my good name
> robs me of that which not enriches him
> and makes me poor indeed.'

It was in the mid-sixties when our family took the first step to establishing a foothold in Bariloche. In those days, the paved road reached only halfway to the lakes and the journey by car from Buenos Aires to Bariloche was regarded as quite a daring expedition. When we set out in a heavily-loaded station wagon, the neighbours gathered to wave us goodbye and wish us luck. They seemed to be thinking: 'What a pity! They seemed quite nice people, too!' They had seen us loading the car and could be forgiven for thinking we were going to the uttermost ends of the earth. Apart from the suitcases, the tent and normal camping equipment, we had kerosene flares, chains, nylon ropes, several cans of oil, fishing tackle, two crates of food, an inflatable dinghy, three spare tyres, a large variety of car spare parts, two fifty-litre containers, one with water and the other gasoline, and whatever else might help us to survive if we were to break down far away in some wilderness.

We crossed the Province of Buenos Aires, a long stretch which to the local traveller usually seems absolutely boring and featureless. To anyone accustomed to the smaller scale of say, Europe, however, the impression is of unlimited space, with the horizon out of reach, beyond an ocean of gold and green. At that time, the great wheatfields were rapidly being harvested and the acres of sunflowers looked like outsize flower gardens. These fertile lands gradually give place to salt flats and scrub up to the River Colorado, then we crossed another arid plain over a road presumably built by direct descendants of the ancient Romans – not a single bend in 100 miles. It was a hot, windswept desert of low vegetation with never a soul in sight, nor a house, nor a drop of water. There were, nevertheless, large contingents of big, furry spiders strolling across the asphalt, provoking some uneasiness and exclamations of surprise from the passengers.

Every now and then on the side of the road we saw little heaps of stones arranged in some kind of pattern and later we learned that this is a very old Indian custom in times of drought, a prayer for rain. There were also occasional wayside shrines and some of them are strange indeed, piled around with bottles of water and dedicated to the Difunta Correa, that is, the Late Mrs Correa.

The legend goes that at a time of local wars and rebellions, she died of thirst in the desert but when found after many days, her little baby was still alive, suckling its dead mother. For some reason, this improbable story was regarded as a miracle by many people and tiny shrines are constructed in lonely parts all over Argentina where devotees of la Difunta Correa leave bottles of water as an offering. The Church frowns on this popular devotion as being completely without basis. Nothing certain is known about her apart from her name – Deolinda Correa, when and where she was born, who was Mr Correa, who found her and what happened subsequently to the baby. It is claimed, however, that she has interceded on behalf of many supplicants in trouble.

The road took us to the River Negro, with its long fertile valley producing especially fine apples and pears, as well as grapes and wine. Lofty poplar trees line all the roads and enclose the fruit farms and vineyards like serried guardsmen protecting the precious plantations from the frosts and incessant, eroding winds of Patagonia.

The journey towards the Andes wound past big oilfields where dozens of scattered pumps clanked up and down like curious mechanical toys. We came to the foothills and the winding stony roads and occasional precipices, until finally we saw the beautiful, peacock-blue waters of Lake Huechulaufquen, surrounded by snow-capped mountains and the 6,000-foot dormant volcano, the great Lanín. Thus began the feast of heavenly scenery which made a lasting impression on us after so many years in the flattest of flat plains.

The Lanín dominates all around it, with its shining crown of ice. It is slightly lopsided and has various features that give the overall appearance of a face whose left cheek has been injured, while two dark depressions look like black eyes. Some say its Mapuche name means 'to have sunk', maybe into sleep or even death, and the local legend about it could be the explanation of this name.

It seems that long, long ago there was a great commotion in this part of the Andes where the resident wicked spirits of three neighbouring volcanoes, the Lanín, the Quetrupillán and the Villarica, engaged in furious combat. The volcanoes flung at each other burning lava, great rocks and deadly flames, while dense smoke and clouds of ash blotted out the sky. The fire burned the forests, the water of lakes and rivers boiled, while toxic gases wiped out all living creatures.

When the battle was over, it was seen that the Villarica was mostly unscathed, although smoke and fire still emerged from it and, to this day, it is active. As for the Quetrupillán, a sideswipe by the Lanín had lopped off its crest, leaving it stunted and humiliated for all time.

The Lanín had managed to preserve its beautiful crest but it had received a ferocious uppercut which destroyed one cheek and other heavy blows had given it two large bumps on the forehead. Nevertheless,

Volcano Lanín

as Gregorio Alvarez affirms in one of his books, *Donde estuvo el Paraíso*, in spite of its battle scars, it has been able to preserve its lordly presence, so much so that the Mapuche God of Creation, Nguenechén, often pauses on its summit to listen to the poets and musicians who rhapsodize over the beauty of the Lanín.

We decided to camp in a sheltered clearing by the shores of Lake Huechulaufquen and began to live our version of the backwoodsman's life. Several miscalculations became apparent as the afternoon wore on and the sun disappeared behind the high peaks. We were alone in the wilds and had expected to reach a camp site several kilometres further along where presumably there would be other campers to keep us company but we had decided to stop in this lovely spot.

As night began to fall we remembered having heard that there were pumas and wild pigs in this region and possibly unscrupulous human beings, so we figured we ought to have two-hour watches through the night.

The two youngest children took the first watch from ten to twelve, they fixed up the fire, wore all the clothes they could find and sat around drinking cocoa and eating sandwiches. It became intensely cold in that unknown grove, where the wind made eerie noises among the great trees and the firelight cast strange shadows.

The children became increasingly uneasy and about eleven-thirty they dived into the tent saying they had seen a white puma padding around. Whether it was a puma or just a dog we shall never know for sure but we like to think that a dog was unlikely so that white puma is now part of the family folklore. Eventually, it was my turn to go out and do a stint until daylight came. It seemed colder than ever but the fire, a couple of blankets, a poncho, innumerable cups of coffee, a pale waning moon and a Chilean radio broadcasting music helped to get the night over.

While on the subject of pumas, it could be mentioned that Argentina has its share of large felines. The puma, once very widespread and still present in considerable numbers, is both graceful and corpulent, with a very smooth, thick hide. It is the 'cat that walks by itself', a great hunter and tireless traveller. It is to be found in varied habitats from the high mountains to the plains, both in arid regions and in humid jungles, although it prefers the transition zones between forests and plains where there is abundant prey and refuge.

After the incident of the puma we decided that discretion was the better part of valour and that we ought to move on to some place where guard duty would not be necessary. We went past a chain of jewel-like lakes in the general direction of San Carlos de Bariloche and eventually pitched our tent by the shores of Lake Falkner, about a mile from a farm where the woods were less dense and the only problem with the local fauna arose from a herd of cows under the care of a colossal Tyrolean bull with horns bigger than our car bumpers. It was the sort of camp site seen on travel posters, rugged mountains patched with snow, around a crystal-clear lake, sunlight glittering through tall trees on to the smooth springy grass and a curl of blue smoke rising from the camp fire.

The whole of this region is a feast for the eyes. The vegetation is as thick as a tropical forest and looks as impenetrable, punctuated by waterfalls and fords. The trees on the Argentine and Chilean sides of the Patagonian Andes are unique to the region, although intimate floristic relationships are to be found with species of eastern Australia, New Zealand, Tasmania, New Guinea and some other points in the Far East. This helps confirm the existence of close connections between these now distant lands in ancient times.

Among the many varieties of interesting trees, a very unusual example is the Arrayán (*Myrceugenella apiculata*), belonging to the myrtle family. It is medium-sized, with shiny dark green leaves and bright cinnamon-coloured bark which peels off in long strips, giving the impression of lianas. In a forest of arrayanes there is an eerie, clammy atmosphere. The trees are cold as stone to the touch and their branches and roots form strange contortions. On the ground lie the remains of other species of trees which have been 'killed' by the arrayán. It allows no other kind of tree to prosper near it, absorbing some sixty per cent more moisture from the air than other trees, thereby gradually depriving them of life. This also accounts for the icy feel of the trunk and the absence of the usual wild life in the wood. In spring and summer they are covered with small, creamy-white flowers, so that the overall effect is very striking.

A large proportion of the trees in the Andean forests belong to the *Nothofagus* family, or Southern Beech, perhaps the most representative being the Coihue (*Nothofagus dombeyi*), the Lenga (*Nothofagus pumilio*) and the Ñire (*Nothofagus antarctica*). Other important species are the Alerce and the Ciprés but these Spanish names are very inaccurate as they are not related to the Northern Hemisphere larch and cypress. The Alerce (*Fitzroya cupressoides*) is an immense tree and can reach an age of over 2,000 years. It is said that some of the *Nothofagus* are unaffected by radiation and that one or two other varieties from the Andean region are being planted in Europe in an attempt to replace the forests devastated by acid rain, in the hope that they will resist.

Today the forests still cover vast areas of mountain land and when we proudly showed them off to my mother, fresh from Europe, she unexpectedly commented that they were beautiful 'but very untidy'. She figured an army of unemployed could profitably be set to work to remove fallen trees and branches (some as big as ordinary trees) and, in general, clean up the borders of the roads.

We were rather indignant at this over-civilized attitude towards our beloved wilderness but she recalled the story of the man working

Road through the beech forests

hard in his garden when the vicar passed by and exclaimed, 'What a beautiful garden! How wonderful is God's creation!'

'Yes, Vicar,' replied the man, 'but you should have seen it when only God worked here.'

At one point in our journey south, the bend in the road took us into a village of a few Alpine-style houses among the trees and a sea of blue, iridescent flowers. It was reminiscent of the bluebell woods in spring in England but the flowers were in fact very tall lupins growing wild, presumably having escaped originally from some pioneer's garden. We also began to notice bushes of wild roses, just like the English hedge rose, growing abundantly along the roadside, evidently another 'immigrant'.

A feature of this region is the disproportionate spread of at least four invader plants, considered a plague by the National Parks authorities and by orthodox environmentalists. They are the lupin, the marguerite, the wild rose and the broom.

The wild rose is a very pretty flower and its generous fruit has for many years provided the basis for home-made and industrial production of rose-hip jam and *tisane*. It has, however, spread aggressively over thousands of hectares of the parks and the countryside in general, menacing other species with its barbed wire stranglehold. Yet around 1989 the one-time pest became the star performer in the rapidly-expanding demand for cosmetics based on vegetables, fruit and flowers. The oil from wild rose-hip seeds certainly does have some remarkable properties. Now a wide variety of brands of oil and beauty creams deriving from wild rose hips is available, with Bariloche at the centre of the activity.

The broom is similarly aggressive in occupying territory but it is more manageable since it has no thorns. In its flowering period in early summer it provides an unforgettable spectacle, an explosion of gold along the roads and mountainsides. As for the lupin and marguerite, they cause less dislocation in the ecological structure and add great splashes of colour to the scene.

The flowers and plants in Bariloche parks and gardens and along the sidewalks are also a source of general admiration. The roses seem to grow effortlessly, superbly and give abundant blooms until the first skirmishes of winter. Before the roses, comes the bright spring chorus of tulips, daffodils, narcissi, snowdrops and lilac which, in the warmer parts of Argentina, do not flourish well. In full summer great beds of a Bariloche speciality, the godetia, invariably draw exclamations of wonder from tourists who go hurrying to the garden shops to buy seeds of this exuberant flower and, of course, other local beauties, while frequently pots of araucaria and pine saplings figure among the returning tourists' luggage. Other Andean towns do not lag behind Bariloche in their lavish displays of roses, lavender and other fine ornamental plants in parks and along the streets.

In March and April the forest of these regions become a magnificent tapestry of autumn colours, while on the higher slopes, dark red patches like stains of spilled wine appear when the leaves of the stunted, high-altitude Lenga change colour, calling to mind the bonny purple heather on Scottish moors.

When at last we reached Bariloche, we were convinced we should try to settle there eventually. Early morning zero temperatures and other lapses in the southern summer tended to cool off the enthusiasm but not enough to change the long-term objective.

A few months later, in Buenos Aires, my husband somewhat recklessly bought a piece of Bariloche real estate at a public auction. The sale was organized by a supposedly reputable firm which, however, had no qualms about resorting to high-pressure publicity methods, so that all manner of solid citizens, many with ample business experience and maybe cautious instincts, succumbed to the seduction of a beautiful introductory colour film with an appropriate Beethovian sound track, exalting the magnificence of the world around San Carlos de Bariloche. When the *son et lumière* died away and the lights went up in the crowded salesroom, bidding was brisk and the lots sold at nicely inflated prices. In subsequent months we learned that he had bought a lovely site with stupendous scenery all around. A few others who had been equally reckless were not so lucky and found they had acquired a hundred-foot precipice, or a lagoon which dries out in summer and fills up with water in winter.

The following summer when we went to visit our site, we met the road builders working at top speed to bring the paved surface right to the Lakes. The road continued climbing, descending and twisting so much that it felt as if it would be necessary to come back the same way to get unwound. The road signs were mostly about the 'sinuous road' and since it is difficult to get up any speed no matter how powerful the car, everyone gets a chance to appreciate the loveliness all around, except possibly the driver. I say 'possibly the driver' because our chauffeur never seemed to miss a view. Hence another family joke: Pa's Famous Last Words: 'Look at that view!'

On one particularly tricky triple-S bend, we came bonnet to bonnet with a large excursion bus. It took some time to squeeze past each other and our youngest boy, who was sitting in front, found himself looking up at the passenger in the first seat of the bus, his German teacher. He waved and grinned as if he were delighted to see her, meanwhile muttering that the sight of *die alte Gans* had ruined his day.

Once in Bariloche, we hurried off to see our piece of ground and decided it was more than satisfactory. We camped at the lakeside among the rose bushes and wild strawberries. The weather was perfect and when the stars came out we saw them with such purity and clarity it was as if we had never seen them before. We watched a couple of satellites but saw no Unidentified Flying Objects. We heard a lot of Unidentified Funny Noises at night among the trees and across the lake but otherwise it was a scene of utter peace.

On recalling the impact this pristine, unpolluted region made on us, I am reminded of a visit, many years later, by my sister who lives in Switzerland. She is, naturally enough, very familiar with lovely mountain scenery, but a trip to Lake Traful, not so far from Bariloche, made a lasting impression on her. In her own words: 'The water seemed to me so wonderful as if the world had only just begun.'

The year after our visit to the site we arranged to have a small house built there and the following year we inaugurated it for our first comfortable vacation without tents and camp fires. A few more years were to pass until we could muster enough courage to burn our bridges in Buenos Aires, to say goodbye to the lovely garden, the family and friends and start again from scratch at a rather late stage in life. My feeling was that some people regarded us with envy but most had serious misgivings, even to the extent of exclaiming: 'You're crazy!' but sometimes it is necessary to be a little crazy in the eyes of the world.

Our love affair with Bariloche lasted seventeen years but eventually it became too hard on creaking joints and arthritic knees. It is one thing to be self-sufficient, with neighbours few and far between, rejoicing every day over the beauty right on our doorstep - the wooded mountains, the shining lake and the flowers - but when one is rising 70 the tough climate and rugged terrain become too much. So we decided to move 120 kilometres to the sheltered valley of El Bolsón. Here we live a pampered life, with paved streets and all the urban services, even the newspaper is delivered to the door. We have a nice garden, flat as a billiard table and there are, of course, several neighbours.

Best of all, most of the family lives here and there are nine grandchildren from 5 years old upwards to keep us on our toes. We had been hesitant to give up our 'glorious isolation' but we have been rewarded with the great satisfaction of accompanying the younger generations of the family and of being accompanied. We wonder what the world will be like for these young people in the next decades. Will Patagonia also be engulfed in the polluted atmosphere threatening to envelope the globe?

This little town of El Bolsón considers itself a Non-Nuclear Zone and an Ecological Municipality. It has various groups of citizens participating in environmental problems, urging action against contamination, litter, forest fires and depredation in general. The non-nuclear position is the result of local and other widespread protests against a proposed nuclear waste deposit deep in the mountains not so far from here. The project was cancelled but the population considers that eternal vigilance is necessary.

In this region there is a delightful living relic of the past which has become quite a popular tourist attraction. It is the Old Patagonian Express, a narrow-gauge railroad dating back to the thirties and it connects the isolated communities on the semi-arid steppe between Ingeniero Jacobacci in Río Negro and Esquel in Chubut, a distance of 400 kilometres. The train is still hauled by the venerable Baldwin and Henschel steam locomotives manufactured way back in 1922 in Europe. Construction of the railroad was no easy task, requiring tunnels, bridges, extensive embankments and a total of 620 curves, that is, an average of one and a half curves per kilometre, all done by

Patagonia

Lake Traful

the 'pick and shovel brigade'. The old-fashioned cars have wooden seats and are heated with wood-fired stoves which are also used by the passengers to warm up food or beverages.

The basic intention of this railroad project was to handle the production of the very large sheep ranches, mainly British-owned and covering thousands of hectares, although now belonging to Benetton. The fact that it served as practically the only means of communication for the lonely inhabitants of the area was secondary but it still serves them today and in addition, it has acquired fame in the tourist industry. Groups of nostalgic retired U.S. and European railroadmen come to ride the ancient steam train and marvel at the ingenuity of the artisan-mechanics who somehow manage to keep the machines going, often creating spare parts long out of existence.

El Bolsón has its history as an outpost of hardy pioneers of many nationalities who, over the years, developed numerous fruit farms especially of hops, raspberries and strawberries, in the wide valley around the town at the foot of the imposing mountain called the Piltriquitrón. This name in Mapuche language means 'hanging from the clouds', while the name El Bolsón means The Big Bag, presumably referring to the shape of the valley. It is obvious that the Indians showed greater inspiration when it came to giving names.

In the sixties El Bolsón became famous, or notorious, when considerable numbers of so-called hippies settled in and around the town. They were not looked on very kindly due to their informal, unorthodox way of life, but they produced attractive, original handicrafts which they sold to the townsfolk and tourists. The hippies are now no more, or else they have become good, solid citizens and they are still very active with their crafts, displayed in the widely-known Fair held twice a week in the main park.

Excursion buses arrive from far and wide and the tourists find themselves tempted with a wide range of articles, from wood carvings, ceramics of many kinds, local wool products, organically-grown vegetables and plants, home-made pies, waffles, cheeses and cakes, to bijouterie and hand-made leather sandals and jackets – the variety seems endless. The organizers of the Fair keep a close watch on quality and try to maintain the highest possible standards to protect their good name.

Patagonia

The region around El Bolsón is yet another example of the beauties of the South Andean lakeland, attracting increasing numbers of tourists. With the unhappy example of depradatory tourism in other parts always in mind, the accent here is placed on variations of the theme: adventure tours on horseback or hiking over mountain trails, visits to the fruit and dairy farms included in excursions, climbing, fishing, bathing in the lakes and streams and, in the season, skiing at the nearby winter resort of Perito Moreno.

So it has been quite a long journey to this land of mountains and lakes, with its pure air and limpid waters, where we are assured that this is where Paradise used to be. I know the Irish claim that Killarney was the earthly Eden, while still others contend that the honour belongs to the South Sea Islands. Naturally, we hope to reach the true Paradise one day, where smog and pollution destroy not, nor outsize corporations break in and devour, but in the meantime, here in the back of beyond, my final appraisal is short and sweet:

No regrets!

REFERENCES

ALVAREZ, Gregorio: *El Tronco de Oro.* Siringa Libros, Neuquén, Argentina. 3rd Edition, 1984.
ALVAREZ, Gregorio: *Dondo estuvo el Paraíso.* Siringa Libros, Neuquén, Argentina, 1984.
BADEN-POWELL, Robert S.S. *Scouting for Boys.* 1908. C. Arthur Pearson Ltd., London, England. 32nd Edition, 1960.
BIANCO, Enzo: *El Enfermero Santo de la Patagonia.* Instituto Don Bosco, Viedma, Argentina, 1983.
BISCHOFF, Efrain U. *El Cura Brochero, un Obrero de Dios.* Editorial Plus Ultra, Buenos Aires, Argentina, 1977.
BONDEL, C.S. *Tierra del Fuego (Argentina): La organización de su Espacio.* Ed. CADIC, Ushuaia, Argentina, 1985.
CAPRA, Fritjof: *The Tao of Physics.* Bantam Books, New York, USA, 1976.
CARSON, Rachel: *Silent Spring.* 1962.
CASTELLANOS, Alfredo: *Cuenca Potamográfica del Río de la Plata.* Geografía de la República Argentina. Buenos Aires, Argentina, 1965.
CASTELLANOS ESQUIU, Francisco: *Fray Mamerto Esquiú.* Editorial Difusión, Buenos Aires, Argentina, 1955.
CELULOSA S.A. Libro del Arbol, Vols. 1 and 2, Buenos Aires, Argentina, 1973 and 1975.
DIMITRI, Milán Jorge: *Pequeña Flora Illustrada de los Parques Nacionales Andino-Patagónicos* (Separata de Anales de Parques Nacionales, Tomo XIII, p.1-222, 1974). Argentina.
DE ERCILLA Y ZUÑIGA, Alonso: *La Araucana, The Epic of Chile.* English version by Walter Owen, Buenos Aires, Argentina, 1945.
FAUNA ARGENTINA, Centro Editor de América Latina, Buenos Aires, Argentina, 1983.

GIONO, Jean: *El Sembrador de Arboles.* Foro del Desarrollo. United Nations University, Tokyo, Japan, 1982.
HUDSON, W.H. *Allá Lejos y Hace Tiempo.* Editorial Peuser Ltda., Buenos Aires, Argentina, 1942.
HUDSON, W.H. *Birds of La Plata.* E.P. Dutton & Co., New York, USA, 1920.
HUDSON, W.H. *Días de ocio en la Patagonia.* Agencia General de Publicaciones S.A.E.y C., Buenos Aires, Argentina, 1956.
JURADO, Alicia: *El Escocés Errante.* Emecé Editores S.A., Buenos Aires, 1978.
KOKOT de AVILA, Johanna: *Extraños Injertos en el Arbol Patagónico.* Ediciones AMARU, Buenos Aires, Argentina, 1991.
KOROL, Juan Carlos and SABATO, Hilda: *Cómo fue la inmigración irlandesa en Argentina.* Editorial Plus Ultra, Buenos Aires, Argentina, 1981.
LEWIN, Boleslao: *¿Quién fue el Conquistador Patagónico, Julio Popper?* Editorial Plus Ultra, Buenos Aires, Argentina, 1974.
MALLMANN, C.A. *Ideas Básicas para una Ley sobre Remuneración del Trabajo en el Hogar.* Fundación Bariloche, Bariloche, Argentina, November 1973.
MARISCOTTI, Mario: *El Secreto Atómico de la Isla Huemul.* Sudamericana/Planeta (Editores) S.A., Buenos Aires, Argentina, 1985.
MILLER, Casey and SWIFT, Kate: *Words and Women.* Penguin Books, England, 1976.
MUSTERS, George Chatworth: *Vida entre los Patagones.* Solar/Hachette, Buenos Aires, Argentina, 1964.
NEWBERRY, Diego: *Pampa Grass.* Editorial Peuser, Buenos Aires, Argentina, 1953.
OLROG, Claes Ch. *Las Aves Argentinas.* University of Tucumán, Instituto 'Miguel Lillo', Tucumán, Argentina, 1959.
OREJA, Pablo Fermín: *Desde la Cúpula.* Editorial Río Negro, General Roca, Argentina, 1982.
PENDLE, George: *Argentina.* Oxford University Press, England, 1955.
PORCEL de PERALTA, Manuel: *Biografía del Nahuel Huapí.* Ediciones Marymar, Buenos Aires, Argentina (4th edition), 1969.
PRESAS, Juan Antonio: *Luján, la ciudad mariana del país.* Editorial Claretiana, Buenos Aires, Argentina, 1982.

References

ORGANIC GARDENING magazine, Rodale Press Inc., Emmaus, PA, USA.

SABATO, Jorge A: 'La Voz Invicta de Gardel', en *La Opinion*, Buenos Aires, Argentina, June 1975. (Newspaper liquidated by the military government 1976-82, owned by Jacobo Timmerman, author of *No Name, No Cell Number*.)

SQUIRE, J.C. *The Oxford Dictionary of Quotations*. Oxford University Press, England, 1986.

TOFFLER, Alvin: *The Third Wave*. William Collins Son & Co. Ltd., London, England, 1980.

TSCHIFFELY, A.F. *Tschiffely's Ride*. William Heinemann Ltd., London, England, 1933.

YGOBONE, Aquiles: *Ceferino Namuncurá: Redentor de su raza de bronce*. Librería Huemul, Buenos Aires, Argentina, 1968.